CAMBRIDGE
UNIVERSITY PRESS

CAMBRIDGE
Primary Science

Learner's Book 5

Fiona Baxter & Liz Dilley

CAMBRIDGE
UNIVERSITY PRESS

University Printing House, Cambridge CB2 8BS, United Kingdom

One Liberty Plaza, 20th Floor, New York, NY 10006, USA

477 Williamstown Road, Port Melbourne, VIC 3207, Australia

314–321, 3rd Floor, Plot 3, Splendor Forum, Jasola District Centre, New Delhi – 110025, India

103 Penang Road, #05-06/07, Visioncrest Commercial, Singapore 238467

Cambridge University Press is part of the University of Cambridge.

It furthers the University's mission by disseminating knowledge in the pursuit of education, learning and research at the highest international levels of excellence.

www.cambridge.org
Information on this title: www.cambridge.org/9781108742955

© Cambridge University Press 2021

First published 2014
Second edition 2021

20 19 18 17 16 15 14

Printed in Dubai by Oriental Press

A catalogue record for this publication is available from the British Library

9781108742955 Paperback with Digital Access (1 Year)
9781108972611 Digital Learner's Book (1 Year)
9781108972628 eBook

Introduction

Welcome to Stage 5 of Cambridge Primary Science. We hope you will enjoy using this book and find out how interesting and exciting science can be.

People have always asked questions about things they observed and looked for answers to their questions. For example, in Stage 5 you will find the answers to these questions:

- How does the body digest the food we eat?
- Why do insects visit flowers?
- How are sounds made?
- How do satellites stay in orbit?
- How do parachutes bring people safely to the ground?
- What gases are in air?
- Where does the sugar go when we stir our tea?
- What causes the seasons?
- How can mice escape from eagles?

You will work like a scientist to find the answers to some of these questions. You will also ask your own questions to investigate.

We have included a variety of different activities and exercises for you to try. Sometimes you will work with a partner or work in a group. You will be able to practise new skills such as drawing force diagrams, completing a key and using models. As you practise these new skills, you can check how you are doing and also challenge yourself to do better. You will be able to reflect on how well you have worked and what you could do differently next time.

We use science in our lives every day. You will see how science knowledge is important when we discuss issues such as pollution and how we must look after our air and water.

We hope you enjoy thinking and working like a scientist.

Liz Dilley and Fiona Baxter

Contents

Contents

How to use this book

In this book you will find lots of different features to help your learning

What you will learn in the unit

> **We are going to...**
> - learn that some plants have flowers and other plants do not have flowers
> - learn about the stages in the life cycles of a flowering plant
> - sort and group flowers
> - identify the parts of a flower and describe their purpose, or function
> - observe and draw a flower
> - describe patterns in observations

Questions to find out what you know already

> **Getting started**
> 1 Draw a picture of a plant. Colour in the picture. Label the parts of your plant.
> 2 Tell a partner why the plant needs each of the parts in your drawing.
> 3 Does your plant have flowers? Do you think all plants have flowers?

Important words and their meanings

> air resistance | streamlined
> drag | upthrust
> friction | water resistance

A fun activity about the Science you are learning

> **Activity 1**
>
> Your favourite flowers
>
> Work in a group.
> - Look at some pictures of flowers. Which flowers do you like best? Say why you like these flowers.
> - Make a collage or draw pictures of your favourite flowers.
> - Show your collage to another group. Tell them why you like each of the flowers on your collage.

An investigation to carry out with a partner or in groups

> **Think like a scientist 1**
>
> **Collect flowers**
>
> > **You will need:**
> > different flowers
>
> Make sure you wash your hands after touching the flowers.
> - Collect a range of different flowers.
> - Group the flowers according to their size, colour and scent. How many groups can you make?
> - Draw pictures of one of the flowers. Label any parts of the flower that you know.
> - Try to name the flowers.

These questions help you track your progress

> **How am I doing?**
> How well can I: ☺ or 😐 or ☹
> - draw a flower and label its parts?
> - identify the functions of different parts of a flower?
> - record observations in a table?

Questions to help you think about how you learn ————————➤

How did the practical activities help me to understand more about parts of a flower?

What did I find difficult?

What would I like to learn more about?

Look what I can do!

- ☐ I know that some plants have flowers and other plants do not have flowers.
- ☐ I can say what the stages are in the life cycle of a flowering plant.
- ☐ I can sort and group flowers.
- ☐ I can identify the parts of a flower and describe their functions.
- ☐ I can observe and draw a flower.
- ☐ I can describe patterns in observations.

This is what you have learned in the unit ————————➤

Project: How people use forces in my area

In this project you are going to use your knowledge of forces to describe how forces are used in a machine or equipment.

Choose a business, factory, transport or farm to visit in your area that uses a machine or equipment where you can identify the forces.

Here are some examples:

- farm equipment such as a pump or a tractor
- a sewing factory that makes clothes
- a factory that makes car parts or computers or any household appliance
- a bus or train service
- a scrapyard that uses magnets to separate iron and steel from other metals
- a water-purification centre.

Work in pairs or small groups. Decide what you will choose for your project. Ask your teacher if they think this is suitable.

Make a questionnaire with questions to ask on your visit. Questions can include:

At the end of the unit, there is a project for you to carry out, using what you have learned. You might make something or solve a problem ————————➤

Check your progress

1 Arrange these processes in the correct order to draw a life cycle diagram for a plant:

| fertilisation | seed dispersal | fruit and seed formation | pollination | germination |

2 Name two ways in which a fern plant is different to a tomato plant.

3 This drawing of a flower has some parts missing.

  a Redraw the flower and add the missing parts from the list:

- sepals
- stamens
- anther
- ovary
- stigma
- eggs

Questions that cover what you have learned in the unit. If you can answer these, you are ready to move on to the next unit ————————➤

  b Label all the parts of the drawing.

  c Which part of the flower forms the seeds?

  d Name the process by which the seeds are formed.

  e Where does the process take place?

Working like a scientist

We can use five different types of scientific enquiry to find answers to different kinds of science questions.

Research

Sometimes we cannot find the answer to a scientific question in a direct way, such as by doing an investigation or by speaking to people. Instead, we can do research to find the information we are looking for by reading books, using the internet or watching videos. These are all known as **secondary sources** of information. We can use this type of scientific enquiry to:

- find out about new scientific discoveries or discoveries made in the past, for example the discovery of magnetism

- find information to answer questions about different topics, such as which birds migrate to your country each year; compare information from different sources and decide which answer is best, for example which foods contain different vitamins or how plants and animals are adapted to their environment

- find images, such as examples of Earth features, that satellites in space photograph and send back to scientists on Earth

- help us realise that sometimes there is no definite answer to a question, for example why the Earth's axis is tilted at an angle.

Fair testing

In a fair test we change one factor or variable and keep all the others the same in order to try to answer a scientific question. By changing only one variable, we know that no other variable will affect the results of the test. A fair test involves three types of variables:

- The variable we change is called the **independent variable**.
- The variable we measure or observe that changes is called the **dependent variable**.
- The variables we keep the same are called the **control variables**.

For example, in Unit 2 when we investigate which material muffles sound best, the control variable is the source of sound because we keep this the same. The independent variable is the muffling material because we change this from newspaper to bubble wrap to a blanket. The dependent variable is the sound volume we measure, because this changes according to which muffling material we use.

Observing over time

In investigations we often need to observe changes caused by things we do. For example, what happens to water when we freeze it, or what happens when we mix sugar and water? How often we need to observe depends on the changes we are looking at. We can see some changes straight away, such as the change in colour of iodine solution when starch is present. If we observe what happens when we mix sugar and water, we can see the change in a few minutes. The changes to water when it freezes will take a few hours to observe. Observing changes in nature can often take longer. When we investigate what happens when a seed germinates, we will need to observe changes over days or weeks, depending on the type of seed. We will need a whole year to observe the changes that happen as the seasons change.

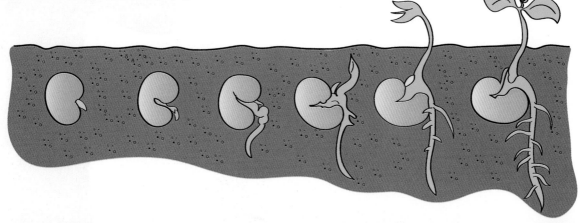

Identifying and classifying

Identifying is the process of naming something, for example an apple or an orange. We can name them because they have features we recognise. Classifying is organising things into groups. We classify objects, materials and living things in groups by looking at the ways in which they are similar or different. We can usually classify these things by asking a series of 'yes or no' questions. For example, does a flower have brightly coloured petals? Does the flower have a scent? The answers to these questions will help us decide if the flower is pollinated by insects or wind.

Pattern seeking

Pattern seeking involves observing, recording and analysing data. The patterns we observe can help us to identify a trend or relationships between one or more things. We often find patterns in nature where
we cannot easily control the variables. For example:

- a pattern in the relationship between seed size and the time it takes a seed to germinate

- a pattern in the type of material that sound travels through best.

> Acknowledgements

The authors and publishers acknowledge the following sources of copyright material and are grateful for the permissions granted. While every effort has been made, it has not always been possible to identify the sources of all the material used, or to trace all copyright holders. If any omissions are brought to our notice, we will be happy to include the appropriate acknowledgements on reprinting.

Cover by Pablo Gallego(Beehive Illustration) *Inside Unit 1* Horst Mahr/GI; Firstbestpictures/GI; Sakhorn38/GI; Claudia Carlsen/Shutterstock; Irina Borsuchenko/Shutterstock; Kissesfromholland/GI; Cezary Zarebski Photogrpahy/GI; Moritz Messner/GI; Mel Longhurst/VW Pics/Universal Images Group/GI; DEA/C.Sappa/De Agostini/GI; Busakorn Pongparnit/GI; Arun Roisri/GI; mikroman6/GI; Peter Cade/GI; Supoj Buranaprapapong/GI; Paroli Galperti/REDA&CO/Universal Images Group/GI; Pal Hermansen/GI; clintscholz/GI; Nobuo Iwata/GI; Soumendra Chowdhury/500px/GI; LilliDay/GI; Joff Lee/GI; Ginet-Drin,Pierre/GI; dcdr/GI; Nick Upton/Alamy Stock Photo; David Tipling/Universal Images Group/GI; Microgen/GI; PatrikStedrak/GI; Dieter Hopf/GI; Sherry H.Bowen Photography/GI; Rodd Halstead/GI; Creativ Studio Heinemann/GI; Afripics/Alamy Stock Photo; Education Images/Universal Images Group/GI; Joff Lee/GI; Ithinksky/GI; atoss/GI; Eisenhut and Mayer Wien/GI; Busakorn Pongparnit/GI; Kateryna Mashkevych/GI; Naturaltexture/GI; Michael Davis/GI; *Unit 2* Steve Bly/GI; Vicki Jauron, Babylon and Beyond Photography/GI; Andrew Lambert Photography/SPL; Peter Dazeley/GI; Fuse/GI; David J. Green - technology/Alamy Stock Photo; Johan Swanepoel/Shutterstock; Ivan Kuzmin/Alamy Stock Photo; andrea crisante/Shutterstock; Wicki58/GI; Oleksiy Maksymenko/Alamy Stock Photo; Kseniya Ovchinnikova/GI; Jmsilva/GI; Inspirestock Inc./Alamy Stock Photo; Kerriekerr/GI; John Lander/Alamy Stock Photo; Image Professionals Gmbh/Alamy Stock Photo; TravelPix/Taxi/GI; Jupiterimages/GI; *Unit 3* Westend61/GI; Luca Calogero Mazzarella/GI; Holger Leue/GI; Tek Image/SPL/GI; Magnascan/GI; Nattawut Lakjit/GI; Membio/GI; Stephen Dorey/GI; Sciencephotos/Alamy Stock Photo; subjug/GI; Cultura/Seb Oliver/GI; Frank Bienewald/LightRocket/GI; Chictype/GI; William Perugini/GI; ajaykampani/GI; chee gin tan/GI; Matt Meadows/GI; AlbertoLoyo/GI; *Unit 4* Nazar Abbas Photography/GI; kyoshino/GI; Keith Brofsky/GI; Burke/Triolo Productions/GI; Claudia Totir/GI; *Unit 5* Prakash Mathema/AFP via GI; Science Photo Library-NASA/GI; Scibak/GI; simonkr/GI; Karol Franks/GI; Grazyna Myslinska/GI; Anne-Christine Poujoulat/GI; Design Pics/Michael Interisano/GI; Richard Clark/GI; DJ Srki/Shutterstock; Ross Fraser/Alamy Stock Photo; CrailsheimStudio/GI; Worradirek/GI; Jeremy Walker/Science Photo Library; Pidjoe/GI; Andrew Holt/GI; *Unit 6* Uniquely India/GI; Photograph by Michael Schwab/GI; Andrew Peacock/GI; Timofey Zadvornov/GI; Song_mi/GI; Bob Elsdale/GI; Mantaphoto/GI; Daniel Dickman/GI; FerryZievinger/GI; Ajay Panigrahi/GI; Rbulthuis/GI; DavorLovincic/GI; Chisnu Phngs Phakdikul/GI; PhotoPlus Magazine/GI; Luke Horsten/GI; Suebg1 photography/GI; Art Wolfe/GI; Designbase/GI; Werner Van Steen/GI; Ariadne Van Zandbergen/GI; DEA/G.Cozzi/De Agostini; Ian_Redding/GI; Jeff Foott/GI; Alexander Safonov/GI; Jeff Rotman/GI; J.Sneesby/B.Wilkins/GI; Life On White/GI; bennymarty/GI; MariuszSzczygiel/GI; zhengzaishuru/GI; arlindo71/GI; ugniz/GI; volschenkh/GI; GlobalP/GI; Jim Cumming/GI; seng chye teo/GI; Minden Pictures/Alamy Stock Photo

Key GI = Getty Images

1 ▶ Life cycles of flowering plants

> 1.1 Flowering and non-flowering plants

We are going to:

- learn that some plants have flowers and other plants do not have flowers
- learn about the stages in the life cycles of a flowering plant
- sort and group flowers
- identify the parts of a flower and describe their purpose, or function
- observe and draw a flower
- describe patterns in observations

Getting started

1 Draw a picture of a plant. Colour in the picture. Label the parts of your plant.
2 Tell a partner why the plant needs each of the parts in your drawing.
3 Does your plant have flowers? Do you think all plants have flowers?

anther	ovary	sepals
carpel	petals	spores
filament	plan	stamen
function	pollen	stigma
fruit	reproduce	
life cycle	scent	

Plants with flowers

Many plants have flowers. They are called flowering plants. There are many different kinds of flowers. Some flowers are big. Some flowers are small. Some flowers are colourful. Some flowers are not brightly coloured. Some flowers have a smell – a scent. Others do not have a scent.

Activity 1

Your favourite flowers

Work in a group.

- Look at some pictures of flowers. Which flowers do you like best?
  Say why you like these flowers.

- Make a collage or draw pictures of your favourite flowers.

- Show your collage to another group.
  Tell them why you like each of the flowers on your collage.

Plant life cycles

All flowers have the same important function. Can you think what it is?

When a plant produces flowers, the flowers usually last only a few days. Then they die and fall off the plant. However, part of the flower stays behind on the plant. This part becomes the fruit. The seeds form inside the fruit. The seeds grow into new plants. The new plants grow and produce flowers to form new fruits and seeds.

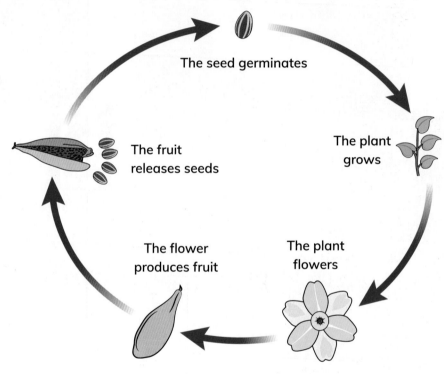

The seed germinates

The plant grows

The fruit releases seeds

The plant flowers

The flower produces fruit

So flowers help the plant reproduce to form new plants.

All the changes in a flowering plant, from flowers to seeds growing into new plants, are called the plant's life cycle. A cycle is something that happens over and over again. There are different stages in the life cycle of a flowering plant.

Plants without flowers

Not all plants have flowers. Plants without flowers are called non-flowering plants. Mosses, ferns and plants with cones are non-flowering plants.

Some non-flowering plants, such as ferns and mosses, do not form seeds. Instead they make tiny spores that can grow into new plants. Other non-flowering plants, such as pine trees, do form seeds. But their seeds form in a cone and not from a flower.

Questions

1 Name an example of a flowering plant that you have seen or know of.

2 Name an example of a non-flowering plant that you have seen or know of.

3 In what ways are flowering plants different to non-flowering plants?

4 Why don't we usually find flowers and fruits on a peach tree at the same time?

5   These are the stages in the life cycle of a bean plant:

flower   seedling   bean pod   adult plant   seed

The stages are in the wrong order. Put them in the right order
and draw the life cycle of the bean plant with labels.

6   Why do we make life cycle drawings in a circle?

Think like a scientist 1

Collect flowers

You will need:
different flowers

Make sure you wash your hands after touching the flowers.

- Collect a range of different flowers.
- Group the flowers according to their size, colour and scent.
  How many groups can you make?
- Draw pictures of one of the flowers.
  Label any parts of the flower that you know.
- Try to name the flowers.

The parts of a flower

Flowers have four main parts.
These parts are arranged in
rings, one inside the other.

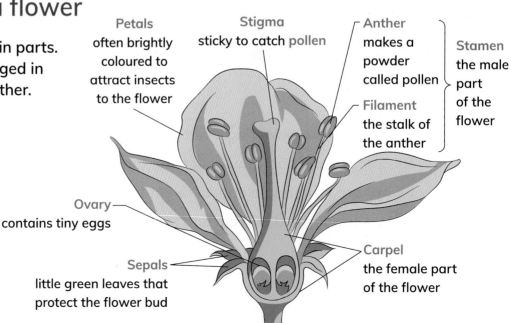

Petals
often brightly
coloured to
attract insects
to the flower

Stigma
sticky to catch pollen

Anther
makes a
powder
called pollen

Stamen
the male
part
of the
flower

Filament
the stalk of
the anther

Ovary
contains tiny eggs

Sepals
little green leaves that
protect the flower bud

Carpel
the female part
of the flower

Most flowering plants have flowers with both male and female parts.
But some plants have flowers with only male parts or female parts, not both.

Think like a scientist 2

Observe and draw a flower

You will need:
a flower, hand lens, tweezers

Make you sure wash your hands after touching the flower.

- Draw the flower and label its parts.
- Count and record the number of petals, sepals and stamens.
  Record the results in a table. Can you see a pattern?
- Carefully pull off the petals and sepals with the tweezers.
- Use the hand lens to look at the stamens and the carpel.
- Find the anthers. Touch their tips gently. What do you notice on your fingers?
- Find the stigma. Touch the tip. How does it feel?

Questions

1 Describe the function of each of these parts of a flower:
   a petals
   b anthers
   c stigma
   d ovary

2 Which part of the flower do you think makes scent?
3 Why are some flowers dark reddish brown with a
   scent like rotting meat? You may need to look for
   the answer in a book or on the internet.

How am I doing?

How well can I:

- draw a flower and label its parts?
- identify the functions of different parts of a flower?
- record observations in a table?

Activity 2

Plan an investigation on flowers

Flower petals are different colours.

- **Plan** an investigation to find out which colour is most common.
- Say how you will present your results.

How did the practical activities help me to understand more about parts of a flower?

What did I find difficult?

What would I like to learn more about?

Look what I can do!

- ☐ I know that some plants have flowers and other plants do not have flowers.
- ☐ I can say what the stages are in the life cycle of a flowering plant.
- ☐ I can sort and group flowers.
- ☐ I can identify the parts of a flower and describe their functions.
- ☐ I can observe and draw a flower.
- ☐ I can describe patterns in observations.

> 1.2 Pollination, fruits and seeds

We are going to:

- draw and label flowers

- identify types of pollination and sort flowers into groups according to how they are pollinated

- say how flowering plants are adapted to attract pollinators

- say how pollination is part of a flowering plant's life cycle

- use knowledge and understanding to make predictions about pollinators

- collect and record observations of pollination in a table

- draw a bar chart of findings

- describe patterns in results, and any results that do not fit the pattern

- do research to answer a question about pollination

Getting started

1   What colour flowers do you like best?
2   Why do you think flowers are different colours?
3   Which parts of a flower make pollen?
4   Why do you think flowers need pollen?

adaptation   nectar
adapted   pollinate
fertilisation   pollination
fertilise   pollinator

Pollination

Pollination is the movement of pollen from the stamen of a flower to the stigma of the same kind of flower. There are two main ways that pollen is moved like this: by insects or by wind.

Pollination by insects

Have you noticed bees, butterflies and other insects on flowers? These insects are called pollinators. Certain insects are attracted to certain types of flowers. For example, butterflies like to visit flowers that are big and have lots of nectar, a sweet liquid. When the insects fly into the flower to feed on nectar inside the flower, they brush against the anthers. Pollen grains from the anthers stick to the insect's body. The insect carries the pollen to the stigma of the same flower or another flower.

Flowers pollinated by insects are adapted to attract pollinators in the following ways:

- They are white or have brightly coloured petals.
- They have a scent.
- They produce nectar.
- They have marks on the petals to guide the insect to the nectar inside the flower.

Pollination by wind

In wind pollination, the pollen blows in the wind from the anthers to the stigmas of other flowers. Grass, rice and corn flowers are wind pollinated.

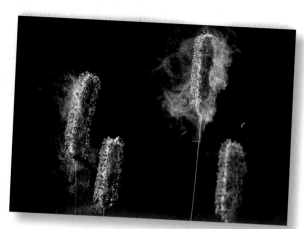

Flowers pollinated by wind have these adaptations:

- The petals are small and not brightly coloured.

- They do not have a scent or nectar.

- They make lots of smooth, light pollen grains that blow away easily.

Activity

Design a flower

- Work with a partner to design and draw a flower that will attract insect pollinators.

- Explain your drawing to another pair of learners.

Think like a scientist 1

Which type of pollination?

You will need:
a hand lens, paper, pencils

- Look at different flowers in the school grounds, the local community park or in pictures.

- Draw pictures of the flowers and label their parts.

- Decide how each flower is pollinated.
  Sort the flowers into groups according how they are pollinated.

- Describe how each flower is adapted to the type of pollination you identified.

- Which type of scientific enquiry did you use in the investigation?
  Say how you used it.

Why must flowers be pollinated?

Plants reproduce by making seeds. The pollen and eggs join to make seeds in a process called fertilisation.

Pollination brings pollen from the male anther to the female stigma. This allows the eggs to be fertilised and seeds to form. Fertilisation happens in the flower's ovary. Fertilisation only happens if the pollen and the eggs are from the same kind of flower.

After the egg is fertilised, the petals and stamens of the flower die. The ovary grows and becomes the fruit. Seeds form inside the fruit. The fruit protects the seed and helps to spread them.

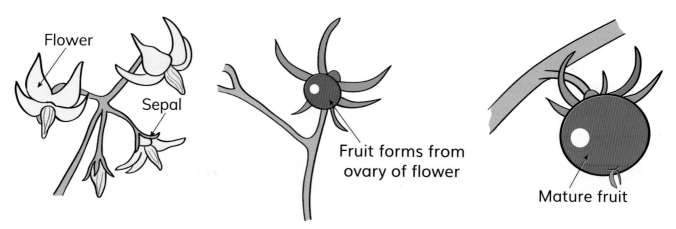

Flower
Sepal
Fruit forms from ovary of flower
Mature fruit

Questions

1 Why do flowers pollinated by insects have brightly coloured, scented petals and nectar?

2 a Why do flowers pollinated by wind have little colour, no petals or scent?

  b Why do flowers pollinated by wind produce lots of dry pollen?

3 How does pollination help the plant reproduce?

4 Explain how pollination is different to fertilisation.

5 a Which part of the flower forms the fruit?

  b What are the functions of the fruit?

Think like a scientist 2

Observing insect pollinators

You will need:
plants that have flowers, a watch or timer

- Find four different plants with flowers.
  Look for flowers that are brightly coloured
  as well as some that do not have bright
  colours, such as grass flowers.
- Observe the flowers.
  What size and colour are they?
  Do they have lots of pollen?
  Do they have nectar?
- Predict how each flower is pollinated.
- Observe which types of insects visit the flowers.
- Count how many times the different insects visit the flowers in half an hour.
- Record your observations in a table like this one:

Name of flower	Description of flower	Prediction of how flower is pollinated	Insects that visit the flower	Number of visits

- Draw a bar chart of the number of times each type of insect visited
  the flowers you observed.
- Name the type of scientific enquiry you used in the activity.

Questions

1 Which flowers did insects visit the most often? Suggest a reason why.
2 Which insects visited the flowers most often?
3 Were your predictions about pollination correct?
4 a What pattern could you observe in the flowers visited by insects?
   b Suggest a reason for the pattern.

Continued

5 a Moths pollinate flowers at night. What colour flowers do you think they pollinate? Say why.

b What other adaptations do you think flowers that are pollinated at night will have?

6 Birds are also pollinators. Do some research to find out why most red flowers are pollinated by birds rather than insects.

How am I doing?

Answer 'Very well', 'Quite well' or 'I need help' to these questions:

- How well can I use my knowledge to make predictions about pollinators?
- How well can I record data in a table?
- How well can I draw a bar chart of my findings?

What did I do to help my group do the practical tasks?

What did I find difficult and what did I do about it?

Look what I can do!

☐ I can draw and label flowers.

☐ I can identify types of pollination and sort flowers into groups according to how they are pollinated.

☐ I can say how flowering plants are adapted to attract pollinators.

☐ I can say how pollination is part of a flowering plant's life cycle.

☐ I can use knowledge and understanding to make predictions about pollinators.

☐ I can record observations of pollination in a table.

☐ I can draw a bar chart of findings.

☐ I can describe patterns in results, and any results that do not fit the pattern.

☐ I can do research to answer a question about pollination.

> 1.3 How seeds are spread

We are going to:

- say how seed dispersal is part of a flowering plant's life cycle
- identify methods of seed dispersal and say how plants are adapted for seed dispersal
- sort seeds into groups according to the way they are dispersed
- observe and make drawings of seeds
- complete a key to identify methods of seed dispersal

Getting started

1   In a group, brainstorm what you know about fruits and seeds.
2   Write your ideas in a mind map.
3   Explain your mind map to another group.

Fruits and seeds

Have you ever swallowed a seed when you were eating an apple or an orange? A fruit is the part of a flowering plant that contains the seeds. Fruits and seeds can be different sizes and shapes. Fruits usually have a skin on the outside, seeds inside and flesh around the seeds.

A fruit has two jobs:

- to protect the seeds inside
- to help spread the seeds.

explode

seed dispersal

seedlings

spongy

Activity

Observe and draw a fruit

You will need:
a fruit, a knife, a pencil, paper

Be very careful when using a sharp knife.

- Carefully cut open the fruit or ask an adult to help you.
- Make a drawing of the cut fruit. Label your drawing.
- Is the skin smooth or rough?
- What colour is the flesh of the fruit?
- Is the flesh firm or soft?
- Is the flesh dry or juicy?
- What colour are the seeds?
- How many seeds can you count? Are there more than ten?
- Are the seeds big or small?

Why seeds must be spread

Have you ever found seeds stuck in your socks? Plants need to spread their seeds away from themselves. We call this seed dispersal. Seed dispersal happens when a fruit is ripe. The seeds are ready to grow into new plants.

Seeds grow into young plants called seedlings. Seedlings need room to grow. They also need light and water. Seedlings cannot grow to be healthy plants if they all have to share water and light in a small area. Plants are adapted to disperse their seeds in different ways.

The pictures show how the fruits of some plants disperse their seeds.

Some seeds are dispersed by animals

Some fruits use animals to spread their seeds. Fruits that spread in this way must attract animals to eat them. These fruits are often colourful, soft and juicy, and taste good. They usually have small seeds. Animals such as birds, monkeys, mice and even elephants eat the fruits. The seeds pass through the animal's body and are dispersed in the animal's droppings. This may be far away from where the animal ate the fruit.

Some fruits and seeds have spines and hooks. These stick onto the fur of animals or the clothes of people.

The seeds can be carried a long way from the parent plant before they fall off, or the animal scratches them off.

Questions

1   Which seeds would grow better: those in a tomato left on the plant, or those in a tomato eaten by a bird? Say why.

2   Do you think peach seeds can be dispersed by animals? Say why or why not.

3   Make a drawing of a seed you think would be dispersed in an animal's fur.

4   How can people disperse seeds?

Some seeds are dispersed by wind

Seeds that are dispersed by wind are light. Have you ever blown away the seeds of a dandelion?

Dandelions have a parachute of hairs to help them float in the air. Other seeds have thin papery 'wings' to help them blow away easily. The poppy fruit forms a 'pepper pot' with holes in it. When the wind blows, the seeds are shaken out and blown away.

Some fruits float

A few seeds are dispersed by water. The fruit must float to carry the seeds away. The fruits have a spongy covering that helps them float. For example, the coconut is dispersed by water.

Mangroves are trees that grow in salty water in warm, wet regions. Their seeds, called 'sea pencils', float upright in the sea until they are washed onto land.

Some fruits split open or explode

Some fruits disperse their seeds by themselves. The fruit dries out and splits open to let the seeds fall out. Some fruits explode and shoot out their seeds. For example, bean pods dry out and explode in hot weather.

Some fruits drop and roll

Some fruits are heavy and round. When the fruits are ripe, they drop from the tree and roll along the ground. If the fruits have a tough outer shell, they may roll quite far from the parent plant. Large fruits that drop from high branches of the tree roll further. Apple seeds are dispersed this way.

Fruits that have a softer skin may break open when they hit the ground and scatter the seeds. Animals that eat fallen fruits help to spread the seeds further away from the parent plant.

Questions

1   A water lily seed has a spongy covering. How does this help a water lily to disperse its seeds?

2   Why are bean pods usually picked before the weather gets hot and dry?

3   Apple seeds are dispersed by the drop-and-roll method. How else can the apple seeds be spread?

4   How are the seeds in this picture adapted for wind dispersal?

Think like a scientist 1

Investigate how seeds are dispersed

You will need:
a variety of seeds, a hand lens, tweezers

- Collect at least five different kinds of seeds.
- Observe each seed carefully with a hand lens.
- Make a drawing of each seed. Label your drawings.
- Say how you think the seed is dispersed and how it is adapted to the type of dispersal.
- Sort your seeds into groups according to the way they are dispersed.

Think like a scientist 2

Complete a key to identify types of seed dispersal

Look at the pictures of the fruits and seeds.
Note the following features of the seeds:

- their shape and size
- the presence of wings, spines or hooks
- how smooth the seed surface is
- the fruit that the seed is inside.

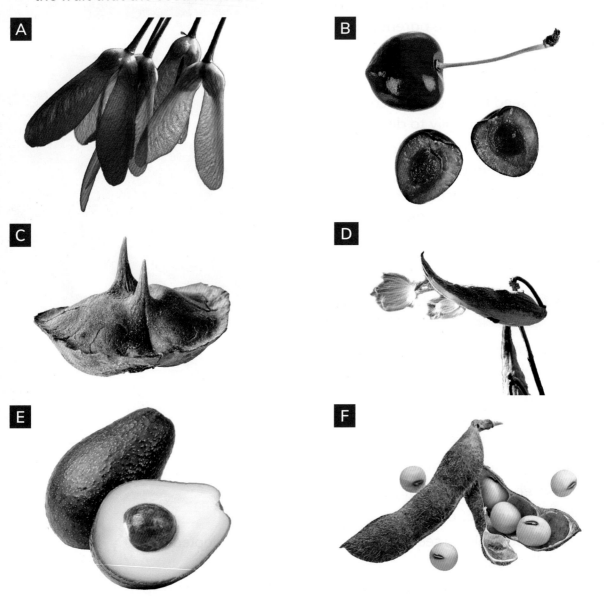

A

B

C

D

E

F

Continued

Work with a partner to write questions to make a key to identify the way each seed is dispersed.

- Make a rough version of your key in pencil. Ask another pair of learners to use the key to see if it works. Make changes if the key doesn't work.
- This could be your first question: Is the seed almost round?
- The last line in your key should be the method of seed dispersal, for example, wind dispersal.

How are we doing?

Answer these questions:

- Did we think of suitable questions to ask about the seeds?
- Did our key help us to identify the methods of seed dispersal?
- Could other people use our key to identify the methods of seed dispersal?

Look what I can do!

☐ I can say how seed dispersal is part of a flowering plant's life cycle.

☐ I can identify methods of seed dispersal and say how flowering plants are adapted for seed dispersal.

☐ I can sort seeds into groups according to the way they are dispersed.

☐ I can observe and make drawings of seeds.

☐ I can complete a key to identify methods of seed dispersal.

> 1.4 Seed germination

We are going to:

- find out what seed germination is
- use knowledge and understanding to make predictions
- identify the conditions that seeds need to germinate
- say how to do a fair test investigation
- record observations in a table
- say why it is better to do the same test with more seeds
- make a conclusion from observations
- understand that we sometimes need to observe over time to obtain results

Getting started

Work with a partner. Imagine a friend of yours wants to plant some bean seeds.

Make a help sheet to tell your friend how to make sure the seeds will start to grow. You can also draw pictures on your help sheet.

| absorb | germination |
| conditions | shrivels |

How seeds grow

Seeds might look dead, but they are not. Seeds grow into new plants. There is a tiny plant inside the seed that starts to grow when conditions – things that affect how something happens – are right. The seed also has a food store.

When a seed starts to grow, we say it germinates. This process is called germination. The seed uses its food store to give it the energy to grow. Before the seed can start to grow, it needs water. Germination starts when the seed takes in or absorbs water. The seed shrivels and becomes small after germination. Here are the stages in germination of a bean seed.

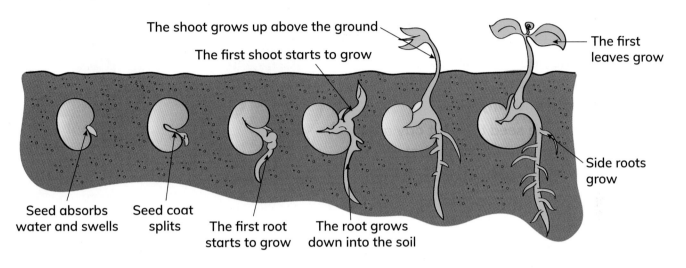

The shoot grows up above the ground

The first shoot starts to grow

The first leaves grow

Side roots grow

Seed absorbs water and swells

Seed coat splits

The first root starts to grow

The root grows down into the soil

Seeds can live without germinating for years until the conditions become suitable. The oldest seed known to germinate was a 1300-year-old seed from a lotus flower found at the bottom of a lake in China.

Think like a scientist 1

Observe a seed

You will need:
a bean seed, a saucer of water

- Soak the bean seed in water overnight. Predict how the seed will change overnight and why.

- Observe the seed the next day and write down any changes that you see.

- Was your prediction correct? Explain why the changes happen.

Questions

1 Why do seeds need to absorb water?

2 a Which part of the new bean plant grows first?

  b Suggest a reason why this part grows downwards.

3 a In which direction does the first shoot grow?

  b Suggest a reason why this part grows in this direction.

4 Why do you think the new leaves start to grow above the ground?

5 Why do you think the seed shrivels and becomes small after germination?

6 Which type of scientific inquiry did you use in the investigation? Say why this type of scientific inquiry was suited to this investigation.

What do seeds need for germination?

Seeds germinate when they have the right conditions.

Can seeds germinate without water or light?

Will a seed germinate if it is very hot or very cold?

Think like a scientist 2

Investigate conditions needed for germination

You will need:
20 seeds, four glass jars filled with soil or sawdust, water, a measuring cup.

Place five seeds against the glass in each jar. Moisten the soil in three jars.

Part A

- Place the jar of dry soil and one jar of moist soil in the same place.
- Check the moist soil every day to make sure it does not dry out.
- Observe the seeds every two days for eight days.
- Copy the table and record your observations.

Dry soil Seed Moist soil

Days	Number of seeds germinated			
	Moist soil	Dry soil	Moist soil in cold place	Moist soil in warm place
2				
4				
6				
8				

Part B

- Place one jar of moist soil in a cold place and one jar of moist soil in a warm place.
- Repeat the steps written in Part A.

Questions

1 Answer these questions for both Part A and Part B:
   a What did you measure?
   b Which factor did you change?
   c Which factors did you keep the same?
   d What difference did you observe between the jars?
   e Suggest a reason for your observations.

Continued

2   Say why it would be better if you had used ten seeds instead of five in each jar.

3   Why did you need to observe the seeds for eight days?

4   Use your results for Part A and Part B to write a conclusion about the best conditions for seed germination.

5   Do you think seeds need light for germination?
    Make a prediction. Say why you made this prediction.

How am I doing?

- Was I able to identify the factors I needed to measure, change and keep the same in the investigation?

- Was I able to use my results to make a conclusion for the investigation?

- Do I know which conditions seeds need to germinate?

Why is seed germination important for our everyday life?

What could I have done better in this topic?

Look what I can do!

- ☐ I can describe seed germination.

- ☐ I can use knowledge and understanding to make predictions.

- ☐ I can identify the conditions seeds need to germinate.

- ☐ I can say how to do a fair test investigation.

- ☐ I can record observations in a table.

- ☐ I can say why it is better to do the same test with more seeds.

- ☐ I can make a conclusion from observations.

- ☐ I can understand that we sometimes need to observe over time to obtain results.

Project: Pollinators and pesticides

This project has two parts.
You must do Part 1 and then choose either Part 2 or Part 3.

Part 1

Read about how pesticides can harm pollinators. Then discuss the questions in a group.

Honeybees are important pollinators. The bees in the picture are pollinating onion flowers. Bees also pollinate the flowers of many other food plants, such as apples, potatoes and beans. In fact, 80% of the plants we eat are pollinated by bees.

Farmers and gardeners like pollinators but they don't like insects, snails, worms and other pests that eat their plants. They often use chemicals called pesticides to get rid of the pests.

Why are pesticides a problem? The pesticides kill the pests, but they also harm pollinators. Pesticides that are sprayed onto plants often cover the flowers. When bees visit flowers to look for nectar and pollen, they take in the pesticides along with their food. Pesticides on seeds can also harm bees. When the seed grows, the pesticide spreads to the whole plant, including the pollen and nectar.

Some pesticides kill the bees. Other pesticides make it hard for the bees to fly and to find their hive or to find other flowers to feed on. Pesticides can also make the bees have fewer young.

How can we help pollinators? We should try not to use pesticides in and around our home and encourage other people to do the same. People should use pesticides only when they are needed, for example if their plants are badly attacked by a pest. They should not use them when the plants are flowering. Some pesticides are sprinkled onto plants or soil as a powder. These pesticides seem to be more harmful than liquid spray pesticides, so people should try not to use them.

Continued

Questions

Discuss these questions.

1 a Bees are pollinators. Name two other pollinators you know of.

   b Why are pollinators important?

2 a What is a pesticide?

   b Why do farmers and gardeners use pesticides?

3 Is it good to use pesticides? Say why or why not.

4 Why is it a problem if bees die or have fewer young?

5 Pesticides harm pollinators.
   How else do you think pesticides can affect the environment?

6 What do you think would happen to humans if there were no more pollinators?

7 Why should people not use pesticides when plants are flowering?

8 Some people use other substances to get rid of pests. Think of, or find out about, other ways to keep pests away without using pesticides.

Now choose either Part 2 or Part 3.

Part 2

Use the information you have read, as well as the ideas from your discussion, to make an information sheet about pollinators and pesticides for people in your area.

Draw pictures or use photos or pictures from magazines to help you tell people:

- why bees and other pollinators are important
- why pesticides are harmful to pollinators
- how to use pesticides safely.

Part 3

Speak to people in your local community who grow plants. Ask the following questions:

- Which plants do they grow?
- Which pollinators pollinate their flowers?
- Do they use pesticides?
- When do they use the pesticides?
- How do they apply the pesticides – in a liquid spray or a powder?
- If they do not use pesticides, how do they protect their plants from pests?

Write a short report on your findings.

Check your progress

1 Arrange these processes in the correct order to draw a life cycle diagram for a plant:

| fertilisation | seed dispersal | fruit and seed formation | pollination | germination |

2 Name two ways in which a fern plant is different to a tomato plant.

3 This drawing of a flower has some parts missing.

a Redraw the flower and add the missing parts from the list:

- sepals
- stamens
- anther
- ovary
- stigma
- eggs

b Label all the parts of the drawing.

c Which part of the flower forms the seeds?

d Name the process by which the seeds are formed.

e Where does the process take place?

4 Look at the picture of a flower.

a What is pollination?

b How is the flower in the picture pollinated?

c Name two ways you can see in the picture that the flower is adapted for its method of pollination.

d Name one other way that the flower could be adapted for its method of pollination.

Continued

5 a What is the process called when plants spread their seeds?

   b Describe two ways that seeds can be adapted to be spread by animals.

6 Copy and complete these sentences about germination.
   Use the words in the boxes to help you.

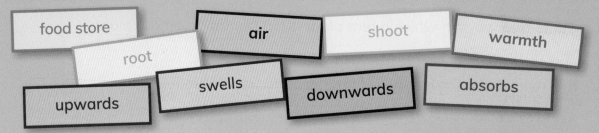

When a seed starts to germinate it _____ water and

_____.

The seed gets energy from its _____.

The _____ is the first part of the new plant that starts to

grow. It grows _____. The _____ grows

next. It grows _____.

Seeds need water and _____ to germinate.

7 Junaid's class germinated seeds under different conditions. These are their results.

Conditions	Number of seeds germinated
Warm, light	10
Warm, dark	15
Cold, light	5
Cold, dark	7

   a Which conditions are best for germination?

   b Do seeds need light for germination? Use the results to explain your answer.

   c Did the seeds get water or not? How do you know this?

   d Junaid must draw a graph of the results.
      What type of graph should he draw and why?

   e Draw the graph for Junaid.

2 Sound

> 2.1 How are sounds made?

We are going to:

- investigate how sounds are made by vibrating sources

- practice observing, pattern seeking and fair testing

- plan a fair test to investigate how well sounds travel through different materials and identify the independent, dependent and control variables

- make predictions using science knowledge and describe the accuracy of predictions, based on results

- choose equipment to carry out an investigation

- decide when observations and measurements need to be repeated to give more reliable data

- describe a pattern in results

- make a conclusion from results making use of what you know about the particle model

control variable	pluck
dependent variable	vibrate
independent variable	vibration

Getting started

1 What is the source of sound in this picture?

2 As the aeroplane flies higher into the air, will Zara be able to hear it?

3 Copy and this sentence and choose the correct word to finish it:

As sound travels further from a source it becomes <u>stronger/fainter</u>.

4 Identify sources of sound in the classroom.

Look at this photograph of a bird singing. We hear the bird song with our ears.

How does sound travel from a source to our ears? Let's investigate this.

Vibrations cause sounds

Sounds are made when things vibrate. A vibration is a very quick movement back and forth. You often cannot see vibrations, but you can feel them. Hold your hand on your throat and hum a tune. You will feel the vibrations and hear the sound.

You can see these guitar strings vibrate when you pluck them.

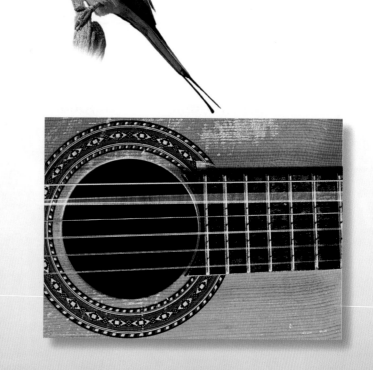

Think like a scientist 1

Investigate how sounds are made

You will need:
plastic wrap, elastic bands, rice grains, an empty glass jar, a metal baking tray, a wooden spoon, a pencil

- Put the plastic wrap over the jar. Keep the plastic wrap in place with an elastic band.
- Sprinkle a few rice grains over the plastic wrap.
- Hit the jar with the pencil. What happens to the rice?
- Hold the tin tray close to the jar and bang it with a spoon. What happens to the rice?
- Predict what will happen if you clap your hands next to the jar. Try it out.
- Was your prediction correct?

Sound travels because vibrations travel

Why did the rice grains move?
Find steps 1 to 3 on the drawing.

3. The plastic wrap vibrates. The rice grains vibrate and you see the rice grains move. You hear the sound.

1. The jar vibrates when you hit it.

2. The vibrations travel through air in the jar to the plastic wrap.

Continued

Questions

1 Did you hear a sound when you hit the jar? Why?

2 Fill in the missing words in these sentences to explain why the rice grains jumped when you hit the tin tray.

Use words from these boxes

| travel | vibrations | air | plastic wrap | rice grains | vibrates |

The _____ travel from the tin tray to the

_____. The air _____ and makes the

_____ vibrate. The vibrations _____ from

the plastic wrap to the rice grains. We see the _____ jump.

How am I doing?

Did this investigation help to convince you that sound travels from a source in vibrations?

Choose from one of these faces: or or 😟

How well does sound travel through different materials?

You have seen that sound vibrations can travel through air and glass and plastic wrap. Does sound travel better through some materials than through others? Let's find out.

Think like a scientist 2

Investigate how well sound travels through different materials

For this investigation you need to choose a source of sound. It could be a buzzer, a bell or a ticking clock. The source of sound will be the same throughout your investigation. This is your control variable.

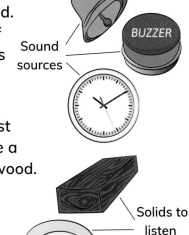

You will test how well sound travels through four or five different materials. One will be air (which is a gas). At least one will be a liquid, such as water, and at least one will be a solid, such as a plastic plate, a metal tray and a block of wood. These are the things that you change. We call the things you change the independent variables.

Work with a partner. One of you can make the sound. The other partner can listen to how loud the sound is through the different materials. The loudness of the sound is called the dependent variable. This is the variable that you are going to measure. Your measurements will be different and dependent on which material you listen through.

- Plan a fair test to find out how well the sound travels through different materials between the source of sound and your ear.

- Predict how well sound will travel through each material you have chosen.

- Draw a table like the one shown here.

- Decide whether the sound is quiet, loud or very loud through the different materials. In the table record how well you heard the sound. Show how loud the sound was each time by using ticks:

    ✓ = quiet   ✓✓ = loud   ✓✓✓ = very loud

- Repeat your test on each material to get more accurate results.

Material sound travelled through	Loudness of sound

Continued

First you listened to the sound through air.

Now I will listen through a different material and tell you if the sound is quieter or louder

Questions

1   Identify your control variable. How did you keep this the same throughout the investigation?

2   Identify your independent and dependent variables.

3   How did you make the investigation a fair test?

4   Which material did you hear the sound best through? Was this what you predicted?

5   Describe a pattern in your results.

6   Discuss in class the reason for the pattern you see.

How am I doing?

Answer 'Yes', 'I'm not confident yet' or 'I need more practice' to these questions:

•   Can I identify the control, dependent and independent variables?

•   Can I plan and carry out a fair test?

•   Can I record results in a table?

Did the activities in this topic help you to understand how sound travels?

Look what I can do!

- ☐ I can see how sounds are made by vibrating sources.
- ☐ I can practice observing, pattern seeking and fair testing.
- ☐ I can make predictions using science knowledge and decide whether predictions were correct or not.
- ☐ I can plan a fair test and identify the dependent, independent and control variables.
- ☐ I can choose suitable materials to test.
- ☐ I can record measurements in a table.
- ☐ I can decide when observations and measurements need to be repeated to give more reliable data.
- ☐ I can identify a pattern in results and use knowledge about the particle model to conclude that sound travels best through solids.

> 2.2 Volume and pitch

We are going to:

- describe sounds in terms of high or low pitch and loud or quiet volume

- make predictions based on science knowledge and describe the accuracy of predictions, based on results

- plan a fair test and identify the control, independent and dependent variables

- take accurate measurements

- repeat measurements for more accurate results

- present results in a bar chart or table

> decibel (dB)
> high-pitched
> low-pitched
> pitch
> sound level meter
> volume

Getting started

These young people are singing.

Describe with a friend how the sounds they make are different.

Volume

The volume of a sound is how loud or quiet it is.

A sound is louder when the vibrations are bigger.
A decibel (dB) is the unit we use to measure sound.

These are the volumes of some everyday sounds.
Very loud sounds (louder than 85dB) can damage our ears.

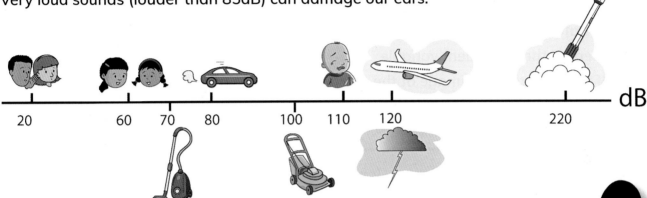

Measuring sound volume

We can measure the volume of sound with a sound level meter.
The meter measures the volume in decibels.

Think like a scientist

Measuring sounds

You will need:
a sound level meter and ways to make different sounds such as
clapping hands, blowing a whistle, slamming a door, the class talking

- Predict which sound will be loudest and which will be quietest.
- Plan how you will measure the sounds. How will you make sure the test is fair?
- Plan how you will record the sounds. Will you use a table or a bar chart?
- Carry out the investigation. Use the sound meter to record each sound.
- Record your results using the method that you chose.

Continued

Questions

1 Which sound was loudest?
2 Which sound was quietest?
3 Were your predictions correct?
4 What was the independent variable in this activity? Explain why.
5 What was the main control variable?
6 Identify the dependent variable.
7 If the singers in the image at the start of this topic sing quietly, how will the vibrations change?
8 Explain why some sounds are loud and other sounds are quiet.

Pitch

Pitch describes how high or low a sound is. For example, a whistle makes a high-pitched sound. Thunder makes a low-pitched sound.

Slow vibrations produce a lower-pitched sound.
Fast vibrations produce a higher-pitched sound.

Some sounds have such a high pitch or such a low pitch that we humans cannot hear them. Here are two examples.

Elephants use very low-pitched sounds that we cannot hear. But other elephants can hear these sounds up to 7.5 kilometres away.

Bats use very high-pitched sounds that we cannot hear.

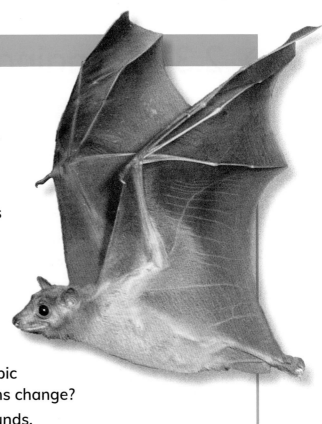

Activity

Sound vibrations

You have seen that elephants use very low-pitched sounds that we cannot hear and that bats use very high-pitched sounds that we cannot hear.

Do some research. Find out which other animals make very high-pitched or very low-pitched sounds we cannot hear. Share your findings in class.

Questions

1   What type of vibrations cause:
    a   a low-pitched sound?
    b   a loud sound?
2   If the singers in the image at the start of this topic have to sing higher notes, how will the vibrations change?
3   Some of the singers make loud, low-pitched sounds. Describe the vibrations that make these sounds.

What do I need to practise more?

Look what I can do!

☐   I can describe sounds in terms of high or low pitch and loud or quiet volume.

☐   I can make predictions based on science knowledge and describe the accuracy of predictions, based on results.

☐   I can plan a fair test to measure different sounds and identify the control, independent and dependent variables.

☐   I can measure sound volume with a sound level meter.

☐   I can repeat measurements for more accurate results.

☐   I can present results in a table or a bar chart.

› 2.3 Changing the volume of sound

We are going to:

- investigate how to change the volume of sounds

- plan a fair test to identify the independent, dependent and control variables

- choose equipment to carry out an investigation

- decide when observations and measurements need to be repeated to give more reliable data

- make predictions and describe how accurate predictions were

- take appropriately accurate measurements and record measurements in tables

- make a conclusion from results using scientific knowledge

Getting started

Look at the picture.

1   Do you think the sound is loud or quiet?

2   What makes the sound louder?

amplifier   microphone

ear defenders   muffle

loudspeaker   silencer

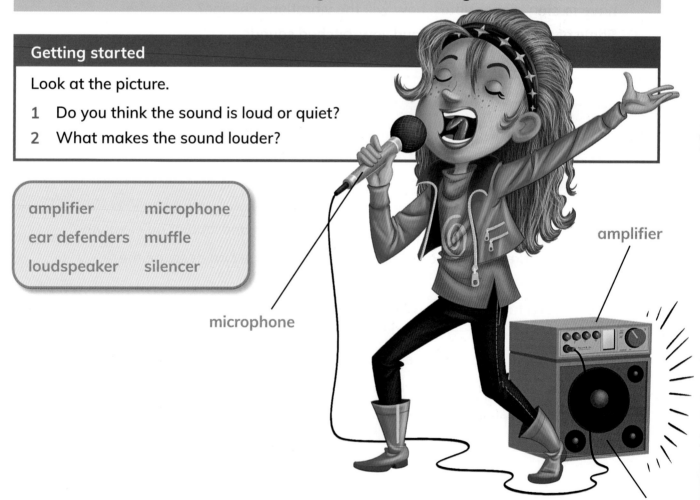

microphone

amplifier

loudspeaker

How can we make sound louder?

In the picture, the singer sings into a microphone. The microphone is connected to an amplifier. The amplifier makes the sound louder. The amplifier is connected to the loudspeaker. The sound comes out through the loudspeaker. The microphone, the amplifier and the loudspeaker make a sound system. This makes the sound produced by the singer louder. We use sound systems to make lots of things louder: CD players and televisions, for example.

Now look at a simpler way of making a sound louder.

Think like a scientist 1

Listen to a sound through a tube

You will need:
a long cardboard tube (at least 50 cm), a source of sound such as a small alarm clock

Look at the pictures. Copy what the children in the pictures are doing.

Hold the clock next to my ear so that I can listen to the tick.

Can you hear the clock now?

Can you hear the clock now? Is it louder or quieter than before?

Questions

1 Identify the control variable. Explain why it is the control variable.
2 Identify the independent variable. Explain why it is the independent variable.
3 Identify the dependent variable. Explain why it is the dependent variable.

Continued

4   Was the sound of the clock louder or quieter when you moved the clock further from your ear? Write a sentence to explain why. Use the words 'vibrations', 'travel' and 'air' in your sentence.

5   Was the sound louder through the tube? Why do you think this happened?

6   Look at the picture. This is the oldest type of music player, with no electronic parts. How do you think the music was made louder?

Activity

Plan a fair test

- Work in pairs. Think of a question about loud and quiet sounds.
- Plan a fair test to find the answer to your question using everyday materials.
- In your plan, list the materials you would use and the steps you would take.
- Explain how you would make it a fair test.
- Suggest how you could present your results.
- Carry out the test and make a conclusion using your knowledge about sound.

Making sounds quieter

Sometimes there is far too much noise. For example, lots of traffic, people sounding horns, loud sounds from construction work and road repairs. Sometimes people near you play music at very high volume. These are examples of noise pollution. Noise pollution has a negative effect on our environment.

What can we do about this? The best solution is to reduce the volume of noise. But if we can't do this we can muffle sounds that we don't want to hear. This means that we make the sounds quieter.

Ways to muffle sound

Loud sounds can hurt our ears. Some people work in very noisy places. They need to protect their ears. They wear ear defenders. Ear defenders muffle sound. What is the source of sound in this picture?

In buildings we use carpets and curtains to muffle noise. Sometimes the spaces between walls are filled with materials that don't let noise through. Walls can be covered with material to muffle sounds.

We fit silencers to cars, trucks and motorbike to muffle the sounds of their engines.

Think like a scientist 2

Find out which material muffles sound best

You will need:
different muffling materials such as newspaper, bubble wrap, a blanket; a source of sound; a shoe box with lid; a sound level meter (if available).

- Predict which material will muffle sound best.
- Place the sound source in the box. Pack one of the materials around the sound source in the box. Then place the lid on the box.
- Stand about one metre away from the box and listen to the sound. Is the sound loud or quiet?
- If you have a sound level meter, measure the sound volume and record it.
- Repeat the activity with the other materials.
- Present your results in a table.

Questions

1 Identify the control variable. Explain why it is the control variable.
2 Identify the independent variable. Explain why it is the independent variable.
3 Identify the dependent variable. Explain why it is the dependent variable.
4 Which material muffled sound the best? Why do you think so?
5 Which material muffled sound the worst? Why do you think so?
6 Was your prediction correct?
7 Is this investigation a fair test? Explain why or why not.
8 Have a class discussion about noise pollution in your community.

How are we doing?

Are you and your partner more confident in identifying the control, independent and dependent variables? Or do you still need more practice?

Did the activity about muffling sound help me to think how I can use these ideas at home?

Look what I can do!

- ☐ I can investigate how to make sound louder and quieter.
- ☐ I can plan a fair test to I can identify the independent, dependent and control variables.
- ☐ I can choose equipment to carry out an investigation.
- ☐ I can decide when observations and measurements need to be repeated to give more reliable data.
- ☐ I can make predictions and describe how accurate predictions were.
- ☐ I can take accurate measurements and record measurements in tables.
- ☐ I can make a conclusion from results using scientific knowledge.

> 2.4 Changing the pitch of sound

We are going to:

- investigate how to change the pitch of sounds
- make predictions and see if our predictions are correct
- describe a pattern in results
- form a conclusion based on scientific knowledge

loosen

stringed instrument

tighten

tune

wind instrument

Getting started

This boy is playing the violin. He changes the pitch of the strings by pressing them.

Listen to some violin music. Talk to your partner. Tell them when you hear a low note, and when you hear a high note. Can you and your partner hear the difference?

Stringed instruments

A guitar is a **stringed instrument**. Some strings are thicker than others. Stringed instruments have pegs that you can use to **tune** the instrument by making the strings looser or tighter. When the guitar is tuned, the pitch gives a perfect sound. If you listen to music and the instrument is out of tune the music sounds horrible.

You can also make the strings shorter by pressing them down. These actions change the pitch of the notes.

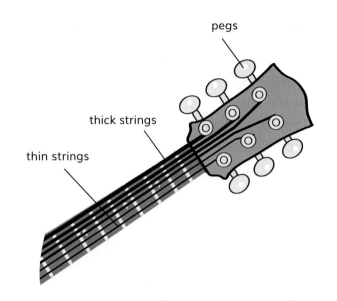

pegs

thick strings

thin strings

Activity

Make high-pitched and low-pitched sounds on a guitar

- Pluck the thick strings and the thin strings on a guitar.
- Which strings make a higher pitched note?
- **Tighten** one of the strings by turning the peg. Now pluck the string. Does the sound have a higher or a lower pitch than before?
- **Loosen** the string by turning the peg the other way. Predict the pitch of the sound when you pluck the string.
- Now pluck the string. Was your prediction correct?
- Now press the strings down on the neck with the fingers of one hand while you pluck the strings with your other hand.
- How does the pitch change?

Questions

1 Copy and complete these sentences by choosing the correct phrase:

The more tightly stretched the string, the <u>higher-pitched/lower-pitched</u> the note.

The thicker the string, the <u>higher-pitched/lower-pitched</u> the note.

2 Are the vibrations faster or slower when you tighten a string?

3 Are the vibrations faster or slower when you pluck a thinner string?

Have fun with wind instruments

Each of these pictures shows a **wind instrument**. Some have one pipe and others have many pipes. People make music from wind instruments by blowing down or across the tops of hollow pipes. This makes the air vibrate inside the pipe to make a sound.

To change the pitch of sound on a wind instrument you have to block one or more of the holes so that the column of air inside the pipe is shorter or longer.

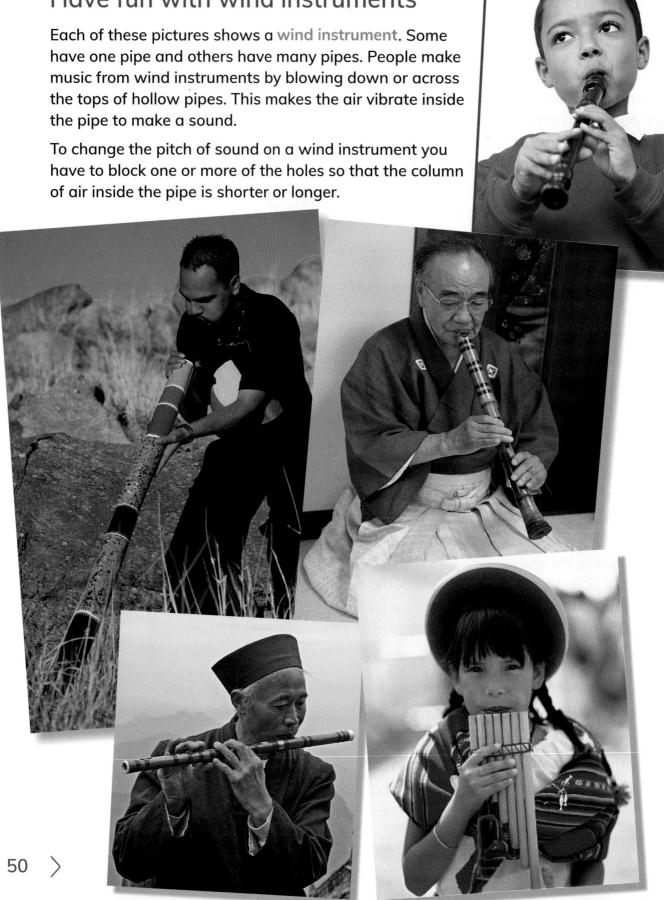

Think like a scientist

Make sounds by blowing

> **You will need:**
> eight glass bottles of the same size and shape, water and food colouring,
> a large jug

- Line your bottles up on a table. You are going to make your own
  wind instrument and use it to change the pitch of the sound.
- Pour water into the jug and colour it with a few drops of food colouring.
  Pour water into each bottle, like as in the picture.

- Gently blow across the top of each of the first three bottles.
- Did you make sounds? Are the sounds from blowing across each
  of the three bottles the same pitch?
- Predict what pitch of sounds you will make when you blow across
  the other bottles.
- Collect evidence to test your prediction.

Questions

1 Write two sentences to describe the pattern of high and low pitches
   and the length of the column of air in the bottle. Use these words in your
   sentence: 'high pitch', 'low pitch', 'long', 'short'.
2 Identify the pattern. Copy and complete this sentence:

   The _____ the level of the water, the longer the column

   of air in the bottle and the lower the _____ of the sound.

Continued

3   Was there a bottle that did not seem to fit this pattern?
    Why do you think that was?

4   Make your conclusion. Complete this sentence:

    The longer the column of air, the slower the vibrations and

    the _____ the pitch of the sound.

5   Why did we have to use the same size and shape of bottle?

How am I doing?

Demonstrate to a sister or brother or other family member
how to make a sound by blowing across the top of a bottle.
Show them how you can make a sound with a different pitch.

Did the bottle activity help you to learn about changing
the pitch of sound on a wind instrument?

Do you think you will listen to music differently now
that you know about pitch?

Look what I can do!

☐   I can demonstrate on a stringed instrument and a wind instrument
    how to change the pitch of sound.

☐   I can make predictions and see if my predictions are correct.

☐   I can describe a pattern in results.

☐   I can form a conclusion based on scientific knowledge.

☐   I can record results on a dot plot.

Project: Noise in my community

One of the negative effects of science and technology is loud sounds or noise. Machinery, traffic and airports all make a lot of noise. This is often an issue in a community. People get stressed and can't sleep properly when there is loud noise.

Work in pairs or a small group. Your task is to find out the sources of noise that disturb people in your community and to find out if anything is being done to reduce the noise.

With your partner or group list all the sources of loud noise in your community that you can think of (for example, traffic, building sites, roadworks, an airport, factories, tractors).

Draw a table listing these sources of noise.

Interview as many people in your community as you can (at least 20). Ask them about each source of noise in turn. If the noise disturbs them put a tick on your table. When you have asked them about all the noise sources on your list ask the person if there is any other noise that disturbs them. Add this to your list.

Present your results in a dot plot.

Choose two of the sources of noise that disturb people the most. Find out if anything is being done in the community to reduce this noise level.
Suggest ways that you think the noise could be reduced.

Present your table, dot plot and
information about reducing noise level on two sheets of A4 paper.

Check your progress

1 Write down whether each of these statements is true or false.

   a   You measure the volume of sound with a loudspeaker.

   b   You play a guitar by plucking the strings.

   c   Low sounds are caused by slow vibrations.

   d   Sound only travels through air.

   e   Soft materials are better than hard materials for muffling sound.

   f   Sound travels best through solids.

   g   Loud sounds are caused by fast vibrations.

2 Look at these pictures of musical instruments.

   A   B   C

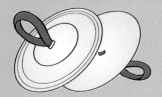      

   a   Which instrument, A, B or C, can you play by:

      i   plucking?

      ii   hitting?

      iii blowing?

   b   How can you make a higher-pitched note with instrument B?

   c   How can you make a higher-pitched note with instrument C?

   d   What instrument could you use to measure the volume of sound these instruments make?

   e   What unit is sound measured in?

Continued

3 Describe each of the following sounds as high, low, quiet or loud:

   a a whisper

   b a bird singing

   c a cow mooing

   d an ambulance siren.

4 Zara and Sofia will use this apparatus to investigate how the sound of the clock ticking travels through solids, liquids and gases.

   a Which container is full of gas? Which contains a solid and which contains a liquid?

   b Identify the control variable, the independent variable and the dependent variable.

   c Why does each container have to be the same size and shape and made of the same material?

   d How will they collect their evidence?

   e What conclusion will they reach?

3 > States and properties of matter

> 3.1 Gases

We are going to:

- learn that some substances are gases
- learn about the particle model of matter for solids, liquids and gases
- find out about the gases in air
- find out that some substances in the air cause pollution
- make a prediction about air pollution
- use results to say if the prediction was accurate
- record results and observations in drawings and tables
- draw a dot plot of results

Getting started

Look at the picture of Zara's birthday party.

1   a   Find all the solids, liquids, and gases shown in the picture.

    b   Write three lists, one for the solids, one for the liquids and
        one for the gases you observed in the picture.

2   How did you decide if something was a solid, a liquid or a gas?

Gases around us

Gases are all around us, for example air. Gases are also in fizzy drinks and inside bicycle and car tyres. We don't always know that gases are there because we can't see most gases. These gases are invisible. We also can't smell or taste many gases around us.

atmosphere   pollute

compressed   pollution

invisible   properties

layer   structure

Activity

Where is the air?

You will need:
a bowl of water and an empty plastic bottle, a balloon or paper bag

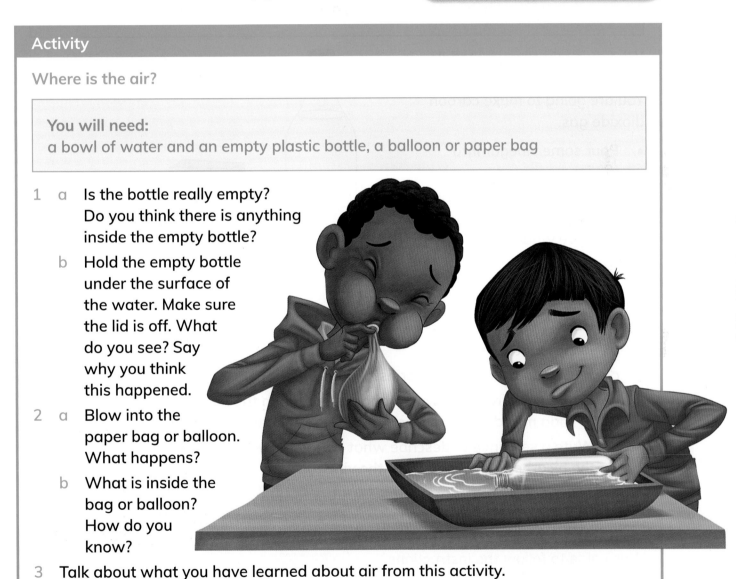

1. a Is the bottle really empty? Do you think there is anything inside the empty bottle?

   b Hold the empty bottle under the surface of the water. Make sure the lid is off. What do you see? Say why you think this happened.

2. a Blow into the paper bag or balloon. What happens?

   b What is inside the bag or balloon? How do you know?

3. Talk about what you have learned about air from this activity.

Sometimes we can see when gases form.

Think like a scientist 1

Make a gas

You will need:
vinegar, bicarbonate of soda, a jar with a wide mouth, a spoon

When we mix some materials, they react to make a gas.
You are going to make carbon dioxide gas.

- Pour some vinegar into the jar.
- Put a teaspoon of bicarbonate of soda into the jar.
  Observe what happens.

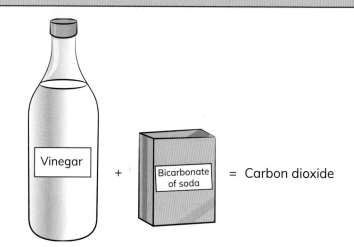

Vinegar + Bicarbonate of soda = Carbon dioxide

Questions

1 What state of matter is:
  a vinegar?
  b bicarbonate of soda?
  c the new substance that forms?

2 a Draw a picture to show what happened when the bicarbonate of soda mixed with the vinegar. Label the liquid and the gas.
  b Write a sentence to describe what happened when you mixed the bicarbonate of soda with the vinegar.

How am I doing?

Point to one of the faces to answer the questions.

 or 😐 or ☹

Was I able to follow the instructions?

Did I observe a gas and draw my observations?

Could I write a sentence to describe my observations?

The particle model of matter

In Stage 4 you learnt that solids, liquids and gases are all made up of particles that move. The particle model of matter describes the structure of solids, liquids and gases and explains their properties.

Solids

In solids, the particles are very close together. There are small spaces between the particles. The particles are packed together in a regular pattern. They cannot move or vibrate freely or fast because they are held together so tightly. They vibrate in a fixed position only. This explains why solids, such as bricks, have a fixed shape and cannot be squashed or compressed.

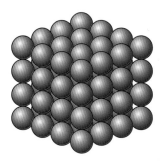

The particles in a solid

Liquids

In liquids, the particles are closely packed but further apart than in solids. There are small spaces between the particles. The particles are not packed in a fixed pattern. Because the particles are not held together so tightly, they can move or vibrate faster and more freely. The particles in liquids can slide past one another. This explains why liquids, such as water, can flow and take on the shape of the container they are in.

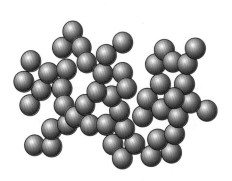

The particles in a liquid

Gases and the particle model

Some substances are gases. In gases, the particles are very far apart from each other. There are big spaces between the particles. The particles can move freely in all directions and move very fast because they are not held together strongly. This explains why gases, such as air, have no shape of their own at all.

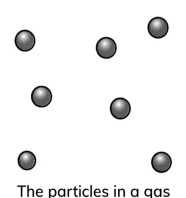

The particles in a gas

Think like a scientist 2

Describe solids, liquids and gases

1   Draw the particle model for each of these states of matter of water:

    a   water

    b   water vapour

    c   ice.

2   In which state of matter:

    a   are the particles very close together?

    b   are the particles very far apart?

    c   do the particles move fast in all directions?

    d   are the particles close together but not packed in a fixed pattern?

3   What does the particle model show us about the structure of solids, liquids and gases?

4   Explain why we can compress a gas, but we cannot compress a solid.

Atmosphere ⟶

Air

Air is a mixture of different gases. A gas called nitrogen makes up about four-fifths of the air.

Air also contains a gas called oxygen. We need oxygen to live. We breathe in oxygen. We breathe out a gas called carbon dioxide, which is also found in air. Air also contains a gas called water vapour.

The layer of air that surrounds the Earth is called the atmosphere. There are many other gases that are not found in air, for example, hydrogen and helium.

Air pollution

It is also important for us to have clean air to breathe. In many places in the world, the air is not clean. People put smoke, dust and gases from factories, power stations, cars, trucks and aeroplanes into the air. These substances make the air dirty and harmful to living things. We say that they cause air pollution.

Air pollution is not only outside. Homes, schools and buildings can also have air pollution. Many things that people use every day can pollute the air. Smoke from cigarettes and cooking, and fumes from spray cans and paints also pollute the air.

Air pollution can make us cough, feel dizzy and give us headaches. People who breathe in polluted air also often suffer from breathing problems. The smoke from cigarettes can cause serious diseases that harm our lungs.

Think like a scientist 3

Measure air pollution

You will need:
five pieces of white or clear plastic, petroleum jelly, a marker pen, a ruler, tape, a box

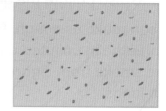

- On one side of each piece of plastic, use a marker pen to mark an area that is 4 cm long and 2 cm wide.
- Label the five pieces of plastic A, B, C, D and E. Then put them in five different places, for example your classroom, the schoolyard, a garage, a park, on a lamppost and in a kitchen.
- Cover the marked area of each piece of plastic with a thin layer of petroleum jelly. Tape the pieces of plastic in place.
- Predict which place will have the most polluted air. Give a reason for your prediction.
- Leave the pieces of plastic for three days. Then carefully put the pieces of plastic in a box and bring them to school. Do not touch the petroleum jelly.
- Observe the amount of air pollution in each marked area.
- Make a drawing of each piece of plastic to show the amount of pollution on it.
- Number the drawings in order of the amount of pollution on the pieces of plastic. The piece of plastic with the least pollution will be number 1. The piece of plastic with the most pollution will be number 5. Write a number under each drawing.
- Record your results on a table like the one below.

Piece of plastic	Place it was put	Amount of pollution observed
A		
B		
C		
D		
E		

Continued

- Draw a dot plot of your results.
- Was your prediction correct? Which place had the most air pollution?
- Which place had the least air pollution? Suggest a reason for this.

Did I do my best?

Did I ask for help if I needed it?

What can I do better next time?

Have I changed any ideas I used to have about gases?

Look what I can do!

☐   I can name some substances that are gases.

☐   I can describe the particle model of matter for solids, liquids and gases.

☐   I can say which gases are in air.

☐   I can understand that some substances in the air cause pollution.

☐   I can make a prediction about air pollution.

☐   I can use results to say if the prediction was accurate.

☐   I can record results and observations in drawings and tables.

☐   I can draw a dot plot of results.

❯ 3.2 Properties of water

We are going to:

- investigate the properties of water

- learn that most water on Earth has dissolved substances in it

- measure temperature

- identify safety risks in an investigation and work safely

- record measurements in a table

- draw line graphs of results

- find information to answer a scientific question

Getting started

1   Have you ever boiled water to make a cup of tea or to cook food? What makes the water boil?

2   How do we know when the water is boiling?

3   What is steam made from? Point to the steam in the picture.

4   Draw and label a picture of water boiling in a pan.

boil	expand	steam
boiling point	melt	temperature
contract	melting point	thermometer

Water changes state

Solids, liquids and gases are different states of matter.
Water exists in all three states of matter. Ice is solid water.
The water we drink is a liquid. Water vapour in the air is a gas.

Water changes state when it is heated or cooled. For example,
when we heat ice, it melts to form liquid water.

When solids, like ice, are heated, their particles gain energy and
start to move more quickly and pull further apart. If the particles
gain enough energy, they move further apart from each other.
The solid becomes a liquid. When a solid changes into a liquid
we say the solid melts. We can show how melting happens
like this:

solid + heat → liquid

If we heat water enough, it will boil. When water boils it forms
bubbles of a gas called steam. Steam is heated water vapour.
The particles of the liquid gain heat and move much more quickly.
Some of the heated particles move far apart and become
a gas. This happens throughout the liquid, not just on the surface.

We can show how boiling happens like this:

liquid + heat → gas

Melting and boiling points

All substances melt and boil. Different substances take different
times to melt or boil because it takes different amounts of
heat for them to change state. The amount of heat in
a substance is called the temperature. We measure
temperature with a thermometer. The unit we use is
degrees centigrade (°C).

Think like a scientist 1

Investigate ice melting

You will need:
a thermometer, a cup of water, four or five ice cubes, a spoon

- Place the thermometer in the cup of water. Wait for about two minutes.
- Measure and record the water temperature in a table like this one.

Time in minutes	Water temperature in °C

- Take the thermometer out of the water. Add the ice cubes and stir with the spoon.
- Repeat the first two steps.
- Measure and record the water temperature every two minutes until all the ice has melted.
- Draw a line graph of your results.

Questions

1 a What did you notice about the temperature of the water up to the time when all the ice had melted?

   b Explain why this happened.

2 a How many minutes did it take for the all the ice to melt?

   b What was the temperature of the water when all the ice had melted?

3 How do you think your results would change if you heated the water in the investigation?

4 Ice melts at the same temperature at which water freezes.
   Why do you think this is so?

5 Which type of scientific enquiry did you use in the investigation?

How am I doing?

Answer 'well', 'quite well', or 'I need help' to these questions:

How well can I use a thermometer to measure temperature?

How well can I record measurements in a table?

How well can I draw a line graph of results?

Like other substances, water needs to reach a certain temperature in order for its physical state to change. The temperature at which a substance melts is its melting point. This is when it changes from a solid to a liquid. The melting point of ice is 0°C.

> Water freezes at 0°C. This means that the melting point of ice is the same as the freezing point of water.

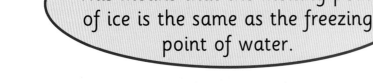

Think like a scientist 2

Is the melting point of ice always the same?

- Do you think ice always melts at the same temperature?
- Are there any factors that can change the melting point of ice?
- Do some research to find out.

The temperature at which a substance boils is its boiling point. This is when it changes from a liquid to a gas.

Melting point and boiling point are properties of substances. They do not change unless the substance itself changes.

Think like a scientist 3

Investigate the boiling point of water

You will need:
a thermometer, water at room temperature, a beaker or small saucepan,
a hot plate or Bunsen burner, tongs

Pour some water into the beaker or saucepan and follow these steps:

- Place the thermometer in the saucepan or beaker of water.
  Wait for about two minutes.

- Measure and record the water temperature in a table like this one.

Time in minutes	Water temperature in °C

- Your teacher will heat the saucepan or beaker of water on the hot plate
  or Bunsen burner. Identify any safety risks that you can think of.

- Measure and record the water temperature every two minutes
  until the water boils. Say how you can do this safely.

- Measure and record the temperature of the water every two minutes
  for another four minutes after the water boils.

- Draw a line graph of the results.

Be careful not to touch the saucepan or beaker or hot water when you
measure the temperature.

Questions

1 a How many minutes did it take for the water to boil?
  b Would the amount of time for the water to boil be
    different if you used less water? Say why or why not.
2 a At what temperature did the water boil?
  b Would this temperature be different if you
    used less water? Say why or why not.
3 What are the bubbles in the boiling water?
  Why do you think they form?
4 The boiling point of pure water is 100°C.
  Did you measure this temperature?
  If not, suggest a reason why the temperature you measured was different.

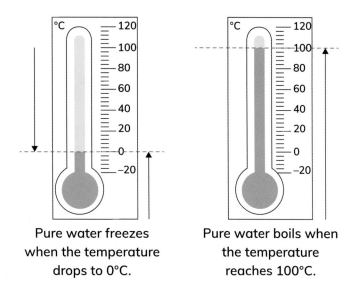

Pure water freezes when the temperature drops to 0°C.

Pure water boils when the temperature reaches 100°C.

The boiling point of pure water is 100°C, but most of our water has small amounts of other substances mixed with it. This makes the water boil at a slightly different temperature. Water also boils at a lower temperature the higher we are above sea level.

Water expands

We know from the particle model of matter that when a substance gains heat its particles move faster and spread out. This makes the substance take up more space. We say that the substance expands. When the substance cools down, its particles move more slowly because they have less energy and move closer together. The cooled substance takes up less space. It gets smaller, or contracts.

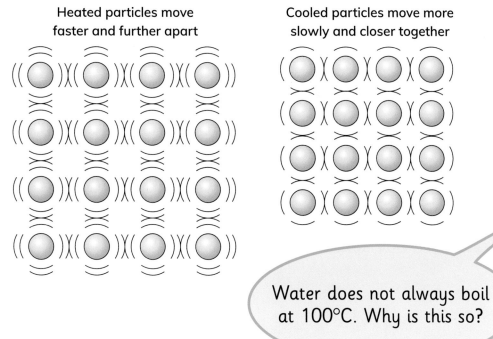

Heated particles move faster and further apart

Cooled particles move more slowly and closer together

Water does not always boil at 100°C. Why is this so?

69

Activity

Observe changes when water freezes

You will need:
a plastic bottle with a lid, such as a milk bottle; a freezer; water

- Half fill the bottle with water. Close the bottle with the lid.
- Put the bottle in a freezer overnight.
- Predict if you think the water will expand or contract.
  Say why you think this.
- Observe the bottle the next day.
  Describe the change that has taken place.

Water does not always behave like other substances.
When we freeze or solidify water, it does not contract as we would expect.
Instead it expands. This property of water also allows ice to float.

How did the practical work help me to learn about the properties of water?

What do I need to practise more?

Look what I can do!

- ☐ I can investigate the properties of water.
- ☐ I can understand that most water on Earth has dissolved substances in it.
- ☐ I can measure temperature.
- ☐ I can identify safety risks in investigation and say how to work safely.
- ☐ I can record measurements in a table.
- ☐ I can draw line graphs of results.
- ☐ I can find information to answer a scientific question.

> 3.3 Evaporation and condensation

We are going to:

- learn about and investigate evaporation and condensation
- use the particle model to explain evaporation and condensation
- use scientific knowledge to make a prediction
- use results to say if predictions are correct
- suggest a way to improve an investigation
- identify variables in a fair test investigation
- make a drawing of observations
- learn about processes in the water cycle
- make a model to show the water cycle

condensation

evaporate

evaporation

precipitation

reverse

water cycle

Getting started

Work in a group.

You will need:
a glass of water, sheet of paper towel

- Dip your finger into the water.
- Make a wet spot on the paper with your finger.
- Leave the paper for a few minutes.
- Pick up the piece of paper and feel it.

Answer these questions:

1 Is the paper wet or dry?
2 What did you do to help get rid of the water spot?
3 If the water is not on the paper, where did the water go?
4 How can what you observed be helpful to people?

Evaporation

When water or other liquids become warm enough, they change into a gas. Water changes into a gas called water vapour. When particles on the surface of a liquid change into a gas, we say the liquid evaporates. Evaporation happens all around us without us noticing it much, like a puddle drying up or washing getting dry.

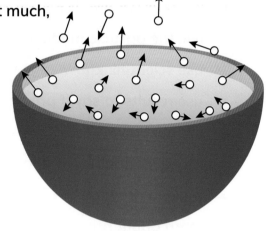

Evaporation happens because some particles in the liquid gain heat energy. The heated particles start to move faster and move further apart. Eventually the heated particles move so far apart that they escape from the surface of the liquid into the surrounding air.

When a liquid evaporates it changes from the liquid state to the gas state.

liquid + heat → gas

Think like a scientist 1

Investigate evaporation

You will need:
two identical glasses, water, a permanent marker, a measuring cup or cylinder

- Measure and pour 100 ml of water into both glasses.
- Mark the level of the water in the glasses with a permanent marker.
- Put one glass in a warm place. Put the other glass in a cool place. Leave the glasses for two days.
- Predict the results you expect to obtain. Say why you made this prediction.
- Mark the level of water in both glasses after two days.

Continued

Questions

1 Was the water level in the two glasses the same after two days?

2 a Which glass had the most water and which glass had the least water after two days? Was your prediction correct?

  b Use the particle model to explain your observations.

3 Suggest a way you can improve the investigation to find out how much water evaporated from both glasses.

4 Why does washing dry quicker on a hot day?

Condensation

Activity 1

Breathing out

Work with a partner.

1 Breathe onto your hand. Does your breath feel warm or cold?

2 a Breathe onto a window pane or a mirror. What do you observe?

  b Why do you think this happens?

The air you breathe out is warm. It contains water vapour gas. When the warm air touches a cooler surface like the mirror it cools down. If the surface is cold enough, the water vapour gas changes to drops of liquid water. The process is called condensation. It is the reverse of evaporation.

Condensation happens because the particles of a gas lose energy when they get cooler. This makes them slow down and move closer together to become a liquid.

Think like a scientist 2

Investigate condensation

You will need:
two identical glasses, ice, water, a measuring cup, a cloth

- Look at the picture to see how to set up your investigation.
- Wipe both the glasses with a cloth.
- Leave the glasses for 15 minutes and then observe them.
- Make labelled drawings of your observations.

Questions

1. a Which variable did you observe or measure? What is this type of variable called?

   b Which variables did you keep the same? What is this type of variable called?

   c Which variable did you change? What is this type of variable called?

   d Was this a fair test? Say why or why not.

2. Use the particle model to explain your observations.

3. Condensation is the reverse of evaporation. Explain why this is so.

How am I doing?

Choose a card to answer the questions.

I get it! I can even explain to others.

I need a little more help.

I don't get it. I need a lot of help.

How well can I identify different variables in an investigation?

How well can I use the particle model to describe condensation?

How well can I say why condensation is the reverse of evaporation?

Activity 2

Make a flow chart of change of state

- Make a flow chart to show the different changes of state of matter.
  Use the words in the boxes.

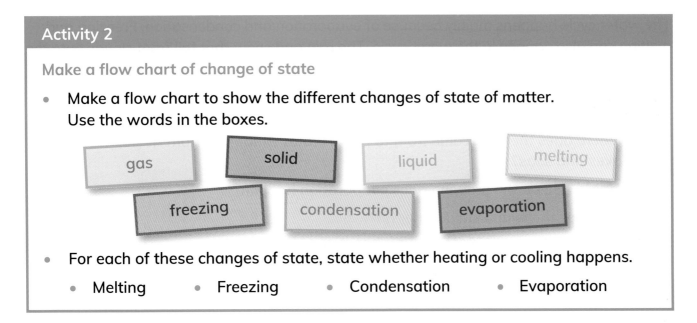

gas   solid   liquid   melting

freezing   condensation   evaporation

- For each of these changes of state, state whether heating or cooling happens.
  - Melting
  - Freezing
  - Condensation
  - Evaporation

The water cycle

Water keeps going around and around in what we call the water cycle.
In the water cycle, water moves from the land and sea to the air and back again.

water vapour condenses to form clouds. Clouds are made up of tiny drops of water

rain falls from clouds

snow falls

evaporation from seas, rivers, lakes and soil

water flows back to rivers, seas and lakes and soil

plants give off water vapour from their leaves

The water cycle happens mainly because of evaporation and condensation. Freezing and melting can also happen in the water cycle. The rain and snow that fall from clouds onto the Earth are called precipitation. Sometimes balls of ice called hail also fall from the clouds.

Questions

1 a Where does the heat come from to make water evaporate from rivers, lakes and seas?

   b Where else on the drawing does evaporation happen?

2 Where does the evaporated water go?

3 a What happens to water vapour when it condenses?

   b Where in the drawing does this happen?

4 How does the evaporated water get back to Earth?

5 Where in the water cycle can:

   a freezing happen?   b melting happen?

6 Complete these sentences about the water cycle.
   Use the words in the boxes to help you.

   a Water on the Earth's surface _____ and moves up into the air as _____ .

   b The water vapour cools and _____ as it rises into the air.

   c _____, snow and hail are forms of _____ that bring _____ back to the Earth's surface.

7 Why is the water cycle important to us?

Think like a scientist 3

Make a model of the water cycle

You will need:
a glass or clear plastic bowl, a small dish which will fit inside the bowl, water, clear plastic wrap or a sheet of clear plastic and an elastic band, a small stone

Continued

- Place the dish inside the bowl.
- Pour some water into the bowl around the dish. The water should be about 1 cm deep. Make sure no water splashes into the dish.
- Put the plastic wrap over the bowl and stick it down. Or put the sheet of plastic over the bowl and hold it down with the elastic band.
- Put the small stone on the plastic. Leave the bowl outside in a warm, sunny place for a few hours.

Questions

1 a Describe what you observed in your model after a few hours.

  b Why did this happen?

2 Say how your model shows the different parts and processes in the water cycle.

What did I do well in this topic? What could I do better next time?

Look what I can do!

- ☐ I can describe and investigate evaporation and condensation.
- ☐ I can use the particle model to explain evaporation and condensation.
- ☐ I can use scientific knowledge to make a prediction.
- ☐ I can use results to say if predictions are correct.
- ☐ I can suggest a way to improve the investigation.
- ☐ I can identify variables in a fair test investigation.
- ☐ I can make a drawing of observations.
- ☐ I can describe the processes in the water cycle.
- ☐ I can make a model to show the water cycle.

> 3.4 Solutions

We are going to:

- **investigate and describe dissolving**

- **decide if a solid is soluble or not**

- **learn that soluble and insoluble substances cause water pollution**

- **investigate how to separate a solution**

- **make drawings of observations**

- **measure liquids**

- **choose and use equipment in an investigation**

- **decide on the type of scientific enquiry to use to investigate a question**

- **learn that dissolving is a reversible process**

- **ask a question to investigate and find the answer**

Getting started

The pictures show different mixtures. How can you separate each mixture? Discuss this as a class.

a peanuts and raisins

b sand and water

c rice and flour

d tea leaves and water

e iron filings and rice

dissolve	pesticides	solute	uniform
fertilisers	reversible	solution	universal
insoluble	soluble	solvent	

Dissolving and solutions

Tea is a liquid. Sugar is a solid. When you put sugar in your tea and stir it, the sugar seems to disappear. You know the sugar is there because you can taste it in the tea. What happened to the sugar?

The sugar has dissolved in the tea. This means that the particles of sugar have spread out into the spaces between the particles of the tea.

Solids that can dissolve in a liquid are called soluble solids. Being able to dissolve is a property of the solid. Not all solids can dissolve. These solids are insoluble.

Mixtures are made of particles of different substances mixed together. Dissolving is a type of mixing because when the solid dissolves it mixes with the liquid. We call the mixture a solution. The solid in the solution is called the solute, for example sugar. The liquid is called the solvent, for example tea. Being able to dissolve a solid is a property of the liquid. A solution will always contain a solute and a solvent.

Sea water is another solution. The salt dissolves in the water to make the solution. The salt is the solute and the water is the solvent.

Many substances dissolve in water. This is another one of water's properties. Water is sometimes called the universal solvent because so many substances can dissolve in water.

Water pollution

Some solutions can be harmful. Some soluble substances can pollute water. We cannot see these substances because they are dissolved in the water, so we don't know that the water is polluted. Polluted water can harm plants, animals and people.

Dissolved chemicals, such as acids, from factories can pollute rivers and lakes.

Farmers put chemical fertilisers in the soil to make their crops grow better. These fertilisers sometimes wash into rivers and pollute the water.

Many farmers also spray chemicals on their crops to kill pests like insects. These chemicals are called pesticides. They can also pollute natural water sources when they dissolve in rainwater and get washed into rivers and the sea.

Insoluble substances in water can also cause pollution. Examples include human body waste, oil and plastics.

Questions

1 What is dissolving?

2 a Can all solids dissolve?

   b How do we know if a solid has dissolved?

3 a Name the two parts of a solution.

   b Give an example of each of the two parts.

4 Why is a solution a mixture?

5 Why is water sometimes called the universal solvent?

6 Why can't we sometimes see water pollution?

7 a Name two soluble substances that cause water pollution.

   b Name two insoluble substances that cause water pollution.

8 How do you think the use of pesticides affects the environment?

Think like a scientist 1

Make a solution

> **You will need:**
> water, coloured crystals, a glass jar, a teaspoon, a measuring cylinder, a watch

Do not touch or taste the crystals.

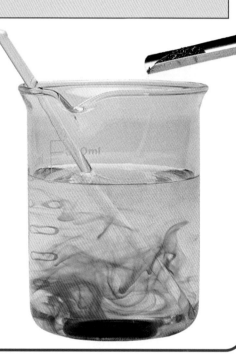

- Measure and pour 100 ml of water into the jar.
- Put a teaspoon of crystals into the jar and observe what happens.
- Describe what you observe in the water around the crystals.
- Draw and label your observations.
- Wait five minutes. Can you see the solid crystals any more?
- In this activity, which substance is the solute and which is the solvent?
- Which type of scientific enquiry did you use in the investigation?

The particles of the solute move between the solvent particles when they dissolve. The solute particles spread evenly in the solvent. Because of this you cannot see the solute in a solution after it has dissolved. We say that a solution has a uniform appearance – it is the same throughout. This means that it looks the same throughout. The picture shows how the solute particles spread when they dissolve in water.

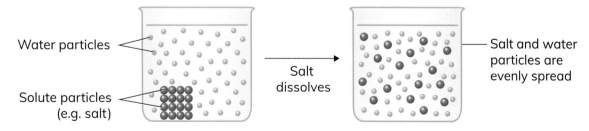

Water particles

Solute particles (e.g. salt)

Salt dissolves

Salt and water particles are evenly spread

Activity

Is it a solution?

1   With a partner, decide if each of the pictures of mixtures shows a solution.
    Say why or why not.

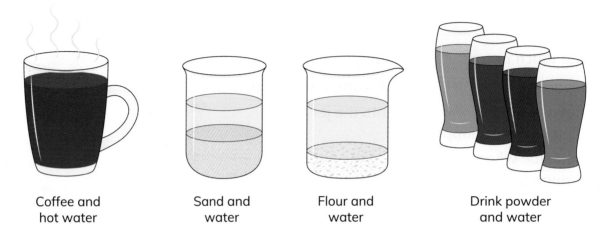

| Coffee and hot water | Sand and water | Flour and water | Drink powder and water |

2   Which substance is the solvent in the solutions?

3   Which of the solids in the mixtures are soluble?

4   What other solutions can you think of?

How are we doing?

Ask your partner these questions:

Can you identify solutions?

Can you say why it is a solution?

Can you identify soluble solids?

Can you think of any other solutions?

Your partner will hold up fingers to answer the questions.

•   1 finger = I can't do it

•   2 fingers = I can do some of it

•   3 fingers = I can do it all

Separating a solution

A solution is a mixture of the solute and the solvent. We can separate most mixtures because the particles of the substances in the mixture are not chemically joined together. Can we separate a solution?

Think like a scientist 2

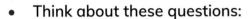

How can we get back the salt?

Most of the salt we put on our food comes from sea water. Sea water is a solution. How can we get salt from sea water? Use your knowledge of evaporation to plan how to get solid salt from a salt solution.

- Think about these questions:
    - What materials and equipment will you need?
    - Which type of scientific enquiry will you use?
    - What will you do?
    - Where should you set up the investigation?
    - How long must you leave it to get any results?
- Carry out the investigation. Make a labelled drawing to show what you used and what you did.
- Make a labelled drawing to show the results of your investigation.

Questions

1   A solution is a mixture. Say how your results show this.
2   Complete this sentence to write a conclusion:
    I found out that it was <u>possible/impossible</u> to separate a solid from a liquid by evaporation.
3   Suggest one way you could obtain results faster.

How are we doing?

Could we choose suitable materials and equipment to use?

Did we work together to plan and carry out the investigation?

Did we use a suitable method to get back the salt?

We can separate the dissolved solute from a solution by evaporation. We call this a reversible process because we can get back the dissolved solute from the solution.

Think like a scientist 3

Ask and investigate a question

- With a partner, think of a question about dissolving and solutions that you would like to find the answer to.
- Decide on the type of scientific enquiry you will use to answer your questions, for example, a fair test, doing research, pattern seeking or observing over time.
- Find out the answer to your question.
- Make a presentation to share with the class about your findings.

What did I learn about myself in the different activities?

Am I happy with the work I did?

Look what I can do!

- ☐ I can investigate and describe dissolving.
- ☐ I can say if a solid is soluble or not.
- ☐ I can understand that soluble and insoluble substances cause water pollution.
- ☐ I can investigate how to separate a solution.
- ☐ I can make drawings of observations.
- ☐ I can measure liquids.
- ☐ I can choose and use equipment in an investigation.
- ☐ I can decide on the type of scientific enquiry to use to investigate a question.
- ☐ I can say why dissolving is reversible process.
- ☐ I can ask a question to investigate and find the answer.

Project: How do people use evaporation?

Evaporation happens when a liquid changes into a gas.

You are going to work in a group to find out how people in your local area use evaporation in their daily lives. You will present your findings in a report.

Step 1: Brainstorm the different ways in which we use evaporation in our lives.

Step 2: Make a list of the different ways evaporation is useful to us.

Step 3: Use your list to make a data sheet to find out from people in your local area the different ways in which they use evaporation. You should speak to ten people of different ages, both women and men. You can add to your list if they name other ways they use evaporation that you haven't thought of. Here is an example of a data sheet.

Do you use evaporation in any of these ways?	Yes	No
1 Drying washing		
2		
3		
4		
5		

If possible, take some photographs to show how people use evaporation.

Step 4: Use your data to draw a graph of the number of people who use evaporation in different ways. Think about the type of graph you should draw.

Step 5: Use these headings and questions to write a report on your investigation. Your report should include your graphs and any photos you took.

Aim: What did we want to find out?

Method: What did we do to collect our data?

Results: What data did we collect and how did we present it?

Conclusion: What did we find out?

Evaluation: How can we improve our investigation?

Check your progress

1   a   Does the diagram represent a model of a solid, a liquid or a gas?

    b   Write a sentence to explain your answer.

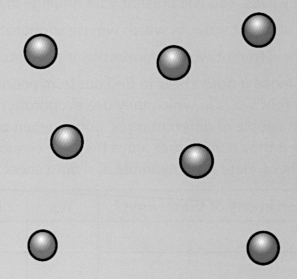

2   a   Name the three states of water.

    b   What is the boiling point of water?

    c   What is the melting point of ice?

3   Write the word that describes each of the following processes:

    a   a liquid changes into a gas at room temperature.

    b   a gas changes into a liquid.

    c   a solid changes into a liquid.

    d   water changes into ice.

    e   heated water changes into steam.

4   Sofia went into the bathroom after her big sister had a bath.
    It was full of mist and the mirror was covered in drops of liquid.

    a   What was the mist made of?

    b   What were the drops of liquid made of?

    c   Name the process that made the drops of liquid form.

    d   Why did the drops form?

Continued

5   When you make jelly, you mix jelly powder with water to make a solution.

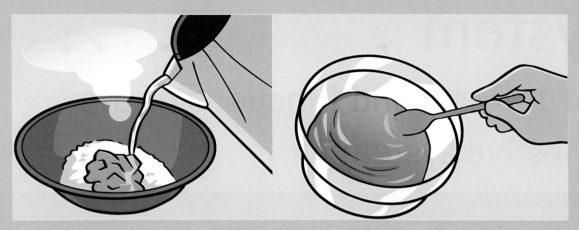

a   Name the solute in the jelly solution.

b   Name the solvent in the jelly solution.

c   Why is the jelly solution a mixture?

d   What has happened to the jelly powder?

e   Make a drawing to show the different particles in the jelly solution.

4 ▸ The digestive system

> 4.1 Parts and functions of the digestive system

Getting started

Work in pairs.

> **You will need:**
> a drawing of a human body outline, coloured pencils or felt tip pens

1 Draw in as many body organs as you can on the body outline and write their names.

2 Can you say what each organ does?

3 Look at other learners' drawings. Add any body organs and labels to your drawing that you have missed out.

The human digestive system

Your body needs food to help it grow. Food also gives you energy. But your body cannot use the food you eat just as it is. Food has to be changed so that it can be used by the body.

The digestive system changes food by breaking it down into tiny particles. This process is called digestion. The stomach and small intestine digest the food. They are the main organs of the digestive system. The mouth also digests some foods. Digested food particles pass from the small intestine into the blood and are carried to all parts of the body.

anus

digestion

digestive system

large intestine

oesphagus

saliva

small intestine

stomach

Digestion starts in the mouth. Your teeth chew and chop up the food into smaller pieces that we can swallow. Saliva makes the food moist which also makes swallowing easy. Digestive juices in saliva start to digest the food.

The food we swallow is pushed down a tube called the oesophagus and into the stomach. The muscles of the oesophagus contract to squeeze and push the food downwards

The small intestine breaks down the food even more until the food particles are small enough to move into the blood.

Inside the stomach the food mixes with digestive juices that turn the food into a thick liquid similar to porridge.

Any undigested bits of food that our body can't use move into the large intestine. The large intestine also absorbs water and some substances back into the blood.

The solid undigested food bits are pushed out of the body as waste

Activity 1

How does digestion happen?

You will need:
a banana, a cracker biscuit, vinegar, water, one leg of a pair of tights with foot cut open, a plastic basin or tray, scissors, a small sealable plastic bag, a newspaper, a plastic squeezy bottle with the base cut off

- Put the cracker, banana and water into the plastic bag.
- Add orange juice.
- Seal the bag and twist, and squash it a few times until the foods are mixed well with the liquids.
- Pour the squashed food into the tights leg.
  Do this over a tray placed on a sheet of newspaper.
- Squeeze the food to the end of the leg.
- Water and nutrients from the food will be pushed into the tray.
  Squeeze until no more broken-down 'food' comes out.
- Put what is left in the tights leg into the wide end of the squeezy bottle.
  Squeeze the bottle hard to push the waste through the other end.

Questions

1 Say which part of the digestive system and digestion is represented by the:

   a cracker and banana   e tights leg
   b water   f tray
   c orange juice   g plastic squeezy bottle
   d plastic bag   h nozzle of the bottle

2 Say how the model is different to the human digestive system.

3 Tell another group how each step matches what happens in the human digestive system.

How are we doing?

Can we explain to others the way the model shows how digestion happens?

Can we tell others if and how the model has helped you to understand the process of digestion?

If the model has not helped us, can we say why?

Questions

1   Why do we need food?

2   Why must food be digested?

3   How does the mouth help digestion?

4   What is the name of the tube that joins the mouth to the stomach?

5   What is the stomach's function in digestion?

6   Which part of the digestive system removes undigested wastes?

7   How does the digested food reach all parts of the body?

Think like a scientist 1

Make a model digestive system

> **You will need:**
> materials such as plastic bottles, plastic tubing, plastic bags, balloons, string, paper cups, cardboard tubes, bicycle inner tube, old pantyhose (tights), scissors, elastic bands, electrical tape

- Design and make a model of the digestive system.
  Your model should:
  - Be made of everyday or waste materials.
  - Show the parts of the digestive system in the correct order.
- Think about the structure and the function of each part of the digestive system; for example, the oesophagus is a long, narrow tube. This will help you choose the best materials for the different parts.
- Place your completed model on a piece of cardboard or hardboard. You can use glue or sticky putty to hold it in place.
- Use your model to explain to a partner how the digestive system works.

Be careful not to cut yourself when you use scissors.

Some foods such as bread and rice contain a substance called starch. We can tell if a food contains starch by testing it with iodine solution. The starch makes the iodine solution change colour from yellow-brown to blue-black.

Think like a scientist 2

Investigate digestion in the mouth

You will need:
bread, an iodine solution, two saucers, a dropper, a spoon

Do not drop iodine onto your clothes. It will stain them.

Do not taste or swallow any iodine as it is harmful.

1 Put a small piece of bread on the saucer. Add a drop of iodine solution.

   a   What do you observe?

   b   What does this show about the bread?

2 Place a small piece of bread in your mouth and chew it. Keep it in your mouth without swallowing it for about three minutes. Does the taste of the bread change? If so, how does it change?

3 Take the bread out of your mouth with the spoon and put the bread on the other clean saucer. Add a drop of iodine solution.

   a   What do you observe?

   b   What does your observation tell you about the bread?

   c   How do you think the bread has changed while in your mouth?

4   a   Is there anything in this investigation that could be dangerous?

   b   Suggest one way you can work safely in this investigation.

5   a   Make a conclusion for the investigation.

   b   Say why you made the conclusion.

Digestive systems of other animals

Many vertebrates have a similar digestive system to ours.
The pictures show the digestive systems of a cat and a rabbit.

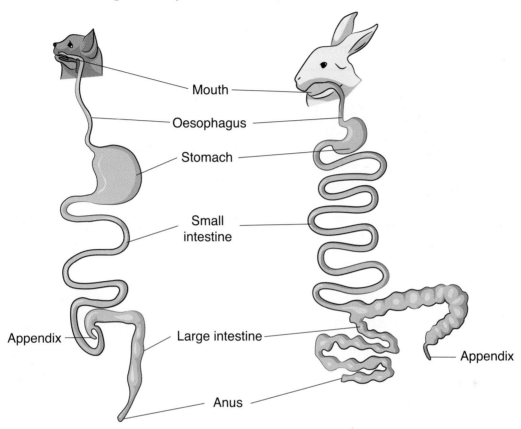

Questions

1   Which parts of the animals' digestive systems in the pictures are the same as the human digestive system?

2   Compare the following parts of the cat and rabbit digestive systems:

   a   oesophagus

   b   stomach

   c   small intestine

   d   large intestine.

3   In which animal do you think digestion takes longer? Say why.

4   Why do you think the digestive systems of the cat and rabbit are different in some ways?

Activity 2

Find out about the appendix

The cat and the rabbit have an appendix. We also have an appendix.

What is an appendix and what is its function in different animals?
Do some research to find the answer.

How have the practical activities helped me to learn about the digestive system and digestion?

Look what I can do!

☐ I can name the parts of the human digestive system and their functions.

☐ I can make a model digestive system.

☐ I can investigate digestion in the mouth.

☐ I can identify dangers in an investigation.

☐ I can use results to make a conclusion.

☐ I can suggest ways to work safely in practical activities.

☐ I can say how the digestive systems of other animals are similar to ours.

> 4.2 Balanced diets

We are going to:

- find out what a balanced diet is and why we need a balanced diet
- draw a bar chart of food groups
- think of a scientific question to investigate and plan the investigation
- choose and use equipment correctly for an investigation
- collect and record results
- write a conclusion from our results

Getting started

1 Write a food diary for the foods you ate at each meal yesterday and today. Include any snacks you had.
2 Which foods did you eat most of?
3 How many fruits and vegetables did you eat?
4 Did you eat any foods you think are not so healthy?
5 Share your answers with a partner.

What is a balanced diet?

Our diet is all the food that we eat. We need a balanced diet to stay healthy. This means we must eat the right kinds of food and the right amount of food.

To have a balanced diet, we need to eat foods from all the different food groups. The picture shows the different food groups and how much we should eat of each group.

balanced diet

carbohydrates

diet

fats

fibre

minerals

proteins

vitamins

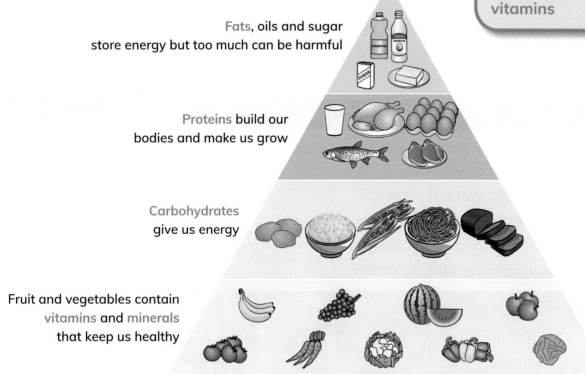

Fats, oils and sugar
store energy but too much can be harmful

Proteins build our
bodies and make us grow

Carbohydrates
give us energy

Fruit and vegetables contain
vitamins and minerals
that keep us healthy

Good and bad carbohydrates

We need carbohydrates to give our bodies energy. But not all carbohydrates are good for us. Sugar is a carbohydrate. Many foods we like, such as cakes, candy and cola, contain a lot of sugar. Too much sugar is not healthy for our bodies. The carbohydrates found in white bread and white rice are also not as healthy as the carbohydrates in wholewheat bread and brown rice.

Questions

Look at the picture of the different food groups on the previous page.

1   Name one food from each group that you like to eat.
2   Which food groups should we eat most of?
3   Which food group should we eat least of?
4   Which food group builds our muscles and helps us to grow?
5   Suggest a healthy school snack that contains a food from three of the food groups.

Water and fibre

A balanced diet also includes water and fibre.

We need water because it has important functions in our bodies. Substances are carried around the body dissolved in water, including water in the blood and other body fluids.

We need water for body processes such as digestion. Water in sweat cools you down. Wastes are passed out of your body in water.

Fibre comes from plants. Your body cannot completely digest most types of fibre. Eating fibre helps to helps food to pass easily through the digestive system. Foods that contain lots of fibre are vegetables, fruits, beans, lentils, brown rice and whole-wheat bread.

Vitamins and minerals

Vitamins and minerals are substances found in the foods we eat. Vitamins and minerals help your body to function properly and stay healthy. Some foods have more vitamins and minerals than others. Fresh foods such as fruits, vegetables, fish and meat contain lots of vitamins and minerals. Calcium and iron are examples of minerals. Calcium makes our bones and teeth strong. We need iron to make our blood healthy. Sodium is a mineral found in salt. Too much salt can be unhealthy for us.

Activity

Talk about balanced diets

Work with a partner.

Make a list of the foods you usually eat in a day. Talk about these questions:

1   Which food group or groups does each food contain?
2   Are there foods from each food group in your list?
3   Does any of the food in your list contain fibre?
4   How much water do you drink each day?
5   Do you think your diet is balanced?

How am I doing?

How well do you understand what makes a balanced diet?
Choose one of these answers:

- I understand this well.
- I understand most of this.
- I do not understand this yet.

Think like a scientist 1

Draw a bar chart of food groups

Zara wants to eat noodles for lunch. She looks at the label on a packet of instant noodles.

1   Draw a bar chart of the different food groups in the noodles.
2   Do you think the instant noodles are a balanced meal for Zara? Say why or why not.

Noodles: Nutrition Information

Food groups in 100g

Protein	10g	Fibre	2g
Carbohydrate	60g	Salt	2g
Fat	15g	Contains 2g of salt	

Think like a scientist 2

Ask a question to investigate

Starch is a carbohydrate. You have found out that starch makes
iodine solution change colour from yellow-brown to blue-black.

1   Think of a question about foods you can investigate using this knowledge.
2   Plan how you would find the answer to your question, and decide which type
    of scientific enquiry will be best.
    a   Which variable will you observe or measure?
        What is this type of variable called?
    b   Which variable will you keep the same? What is this type of variable called?
    c   Which variable will you change? What is this type of variable called?
3   Choose the materials you will use.
4   Decide how you will record and present your results.
5   Carry out the investigation and write a conclusion from your results.

How has this topic helped me to know:
• if my diet is balanced?
• which food groups I should eat more of?
• which food groups I should eat less of?

Look what I can do!

☐   I can say what a balanced diet is and why we need a balanced diet.
☐   I can draw a bar chart of food groups.
☐   I can ask a scientific question to investigate and plan the investigation.
☐   I can choose and use equipment correctly for an investigation.
☐   I can collect and record results.
☐   I can write a conclusion from my results.

Project: Vitamins

Part 1

The discovery of Vitamin C

James Lind was Scottish doctor who lived 300 years ago. A sea captain from that time wrote that on a long sea voyage 380 sailors out of 510 had died of a disease called scurvy. The sailors with scurvy got sores on their bodies. They also had bleeding gums and their teeth fell out.

No one knew why the sailors got the disease or how to prevent or cure it. Some doctors believed that scurvy was caused by food that wasn't properly digested, bad water, too much hard work and living in damp conditions.

James Lind wanted to find out more about scurvy. He read medical reports to find as much information as he could about the disease. He also carried out an investigation. He tested six different treatments on 12 sailors who had scurvy.

Each day two sailors were given an apple drink, two had seawater and another two had a mixture of garlic, mustard and dried radish root. Another group of two were given vinegar, two were given weak sulfuric acid and the last two ate oranges and lemons.

These are Lind's results after 14 days.

Treatment	Result
Apple drink	Some improvement
Seawater	No improvement
Garlic, mustard and dried radish root	No improvement
Vinegar	No improvement
Weak sulfuric acid	No improvement
Oranges and lemons	No signs of scurvy

Lind had discovered a cure for scurvy, but he did not know why it worked. It was only in the 1930s that scientists discovered from their experiments which substance in fruits and vegetables prevents and cures scurvy. They called the substance Vitamin C.

Continued

Discuss these questions.

1   What are the effects of scurvy on the body?

2   What did doctors long ago think caused scurvy?

3   How did James Lind find out more about scurvy?

4   Which was the best treatment for scurvy in Lind's investigation?
    How do you know this?

5   Why do you think the sailors who had the apple drink showed
    some improvement?

6   a   What could Lind conclude from his investigation?

    b   How has our knowledge about scurvy changed since Lind's time?
        Say why this happened.

Part 2

Which foods contain vitamins?

1   Do some research from books and the internet to find out which foods
    contain the following vitamins:

    * Vitamin A
    * Vitamin B group
    * Vitamin C

    * Vitamin D
    * Vitamin E
    * Vitamin K

2   Make a vitamin chart with a title, pictures and labels that you could use
    to tell people about the foods that contain the vitamins they need.

Check your progress

1   Use the words in the boxes to complete the sentences about digestion.

mouth   stomach   small intestine   oesophagus   large intestine

   a   Food is pushed down the _____ into the stomach.

   b   In the _____ the food is broken down into very
       small particles.

   c   The food is mixed with digestive juices in the _____ .

   d   Undigested food is pushed out of the body through the end of the
       _____ .

   e   The food is chewed in the _____ .

2   The sentences in question 1 are in the wrong order.
    Sort them into the correct order of the stages of digestion.

3   Decide if each of these statements is true or false.

   a   We get energy from carbohydrates.

   b   We need to eat fat to help us grow and build our bodies.

   c   Fibre in our food gives us energy.

   d   We can drink juice and cola instead of water.

   e   Fruits and vegetables contain lots of vitamins and minerals.

   f   Calcium helps to make our teeth and bones strong.

4   Arun had noodles, chicken, an orange and a cola
    drink for lunch.

   a   Which food helps Arun grow?

   b   Which food gives him energy?

   c   Which food gives him vitamins and minerals?

   d   Identify two foods he can change to make his
       meal healthier. Give a reason for your answer.

Continued

5   Mrs Pather went to the supermarket. She couldn't decide if she should buy a can of butterbeans or a can of creamed corn. Look at the labels of the two cans and answer the questions.

    a   Which food has the most protein?

    b   Which food has the most sugar?

    c   Name two minerals found in the canned foods.

    d   Which can should Mrs Pather choose as part of a balanced diet?

    e   Explain your answer to part **d**.

Butterbeans		Creamed corn	
Food groups in 100g		Food groups in 100g	
Protein	15g	Protein	4.5g
Carbohydrate	36g	Carbohydrate	38g
Fat	1g	Fat	1g
Fibre	12g	Fibre	3g
Sugars	5g	Sugars	9g
Calcium	80mg	Calcium	8mg
Iron	7mg	Iron	7mg

5 Forces and magnetism

> 5.1 Gravity, normal forces and applied forces

We are going to:

- **identify gravity and normal and applied forces**
- **use force diagrams to show the name and direction of forces acting on an object**

applied force

attracts

exert

force

gravity

normal force

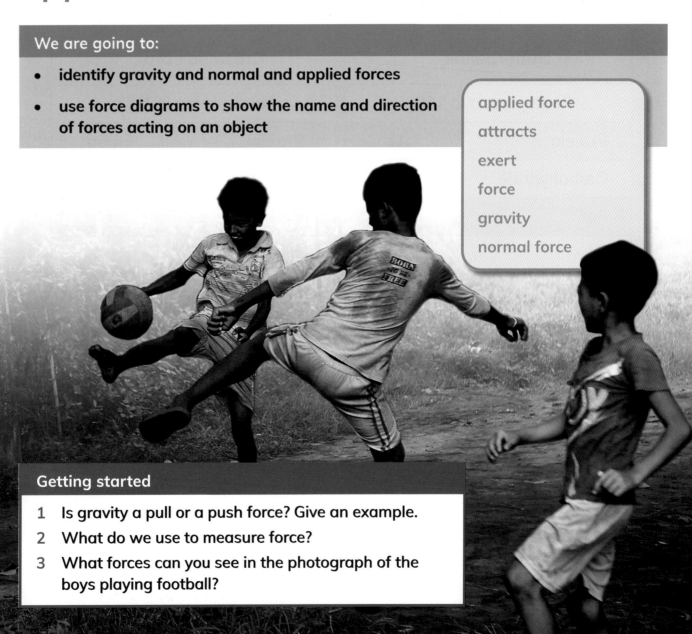

Getting started

1 Is gravity a pull or a push force? Give an example.

2 What do we use to measure force?

3 What forces can you see in the photograph of the boys playing football?

Gravity and normal forces

Gravity is very important to our everyday lives. Without gravity we would fly off the Earth! We would all have to be tied down all the time. If you kicked a ball, it would fly off forever.

Gravity works on both objects at rest and objects that are moving. Gravity is the force which attracts or pulls all objects towards the Earth.

A normal force is a support force. A normal force is made on an object that is in contact with another object. The objects do not move. For example, if you put a book on a table the book is at rest. Are there any forces acting on the book?

The book will make or exert a downward force on the table. This force is gravity pulling the book downwards. But the book does not fall, so something must be pushing it up. This is called the normal force. We can't see these forces at work but we can show them on a force diagram.

Force diagrams

We can show the direction of forces on a force diagram. Each force is shown as an arrow. When the forces are equal the arrows are the same size.

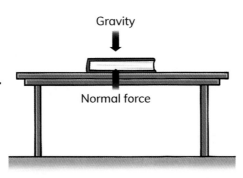

Gravity

Normal force

Forces act in pairs. In the picture, the book exerts a downward force on the table – this is gravity. The arrow shows the force of gravity pointing down. The table exerts an upward force on the book – this is the normal force. The arrow for the normal force points up. The two forces are in opposite directions. The two forces are equal so the arrows are the same size.

Think like a scientist

Using force diagrams

1 How do we show forces on a force diagram?

2 How do we show the direction of the force?

3 How do we show the size of the force?

4 Here is a force diagram of a person sitting on a chair. Which forces do the arrows show?

5 When you stand still, why don't you sink into the ground? Draw a force diagram to explain your answer. Label gravity and normal force.

What are applied forces?

In the photograph at the beginning of this topic, the children are kicking the ball. This is an applied force. In the picture Marcus is pushing the table. This is an also an applied force. An applied force is any force that is applied to another object or person. In this example, Marcus applies force on the table by pushing it.

In this picture, Zara is opening the door. She pulls the door towards her. The pulling action is an applied force.

From these two examples you can see that an applied force happens when an object is pushed or pulled by another object. The other object can be a person or a machine or machine part.

Activity

Identify applied forces

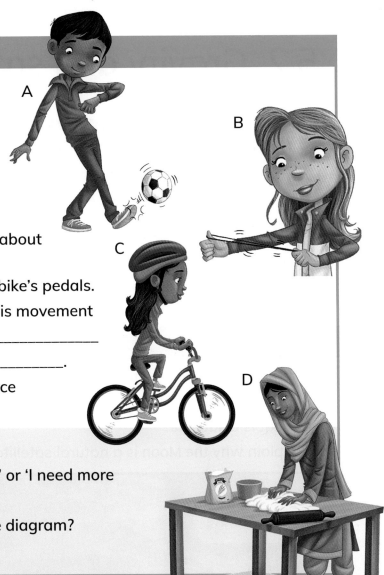

A

B

C

D

1 For each picture, A, B and D:

 a Identify the movement as a push or a pull or both.

 b How do you know these are all applied forces?

2 Copy and complete these sentences about picture C:

 Zara _____ down on the bike's pedals.

 This is an _____ force. This movement

 pulls the chain, which is another _____

 force. This moves the bike's _____.

3 Describe how you use an applied force to get up off your chair.

How am I doing?

Answer 'very well', 'not very confidently' or 'I need more practice' to each of these questions:

How well can I identify forces on a force diagram?

How well can I draw a force diagram?

Did I ask for help if I needed it?

Look what I can do!

☐ I can identify gravity as a force.

☐ I can identify normal and applied forces.

☐ I can use force diagrams to show the name and direction of forces acting on an object.

> 5.2 Gravity and satellites

We are going to:

- identify gravity
- use a model to see how gravity keeps a satellite in orbit
- know that a satellite is an object in space that orbits a larger object
- use a force diagram to show the name and direction of forces acting on an object

Getting started

This photograph shows a tropical cyclone near the coast of Australia. It was taken by a satellite that was made by people and put into space.

1 What is a satellite?
2 Explain why the Moon is a natural satellite.

artificial satellite

How much gravity?

All objects exert gravity. When there are two objects, they exert gravity on each other. The amount of gravity an object has depends on size. The larger the object, the greater the force of gravity. Gravity works over a distance. So the amount of gravity also depends on how close the objects are: the closer the objects are, the stronger the forces of gravity between them. We are going to look at satellites as an example of this.

Satellites

In space, a body which orbits a larger body is called a satellite.

The Moon is a natural satellite of the Earth.

The Moon and the Earth are attracted towards each other by gravity. The Earth is larger than the Moon. So the Earth exerts a greater force of gravity on the Moon than the Moon exerts on the Earth. Look at this model of the Moon orbiting the Earth.

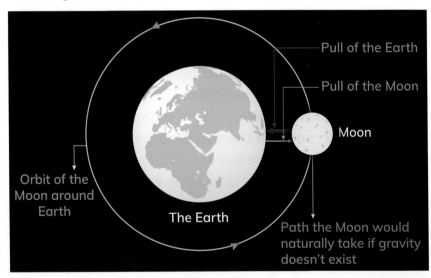

Point to the Earth. Point to the Moon. Point to the Moon's orbit around the Earth.

Find the green arrow. The green arrow shows the force of gravity the Moon exerts on the Earth. Remember gravity is a pulling force so the Moon is pulling the Earth. That is why the arrow points towards the Moon.

Find the red arrow. The red arrow shows the force of gravity the Earth exerts on the Moon.

Think like a scientist

Use a model to understand how gravity keeps the Moon in orbit

1   Which is greater, the pull of gravity that the Moon exerts on the Earth or the pull of gravity that the Earth exerts on the Moon?

2   How does the diagram on the previous page show this?

3   Explain why one force of gravity is greater than the other.

4   What path would the Moon take if there was no gravity?

5   List ways that the diagram is a good model to explain how the Moon orbits the Earth.

How am I doing?

Answer 'very well', 'better than before' or 'I still need more practice' to each of these questions:

• How well can I identify forces on a force diagram?

• How well can I draw a force diagram?

Artificial satellites

Scientists have used what they know about natural satellites to design and make satellites. These satellites are called artificial satellites. There are many artificial satellites which orbit the Earth. Artificial satellites have a positive effect on our lives and environment. For example, some of the satellites continuously take photographs which help to make weather predictions. Other satellites provide TV signals and GPS used on ships, aeroplanes and some cars.

The International Space Station is an artificial satellite that has scientists living on it for years at a time. The scientists carry out investigations in space and use their findings back on Earth.

How does an artificial satellite get into space?

An artificial satellite is launched into space by powerful rockets. The satellite travels at an enormous speed to overcome the force of gravity pulling it towards the centre of the Earth. Then, at a certain distance above the Earth, it keeps moving at the same speed in an orbit around the Earth. Gravity pulls the satellite toward the centre of the Earth and keeps it in orbit.

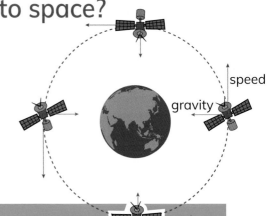

Activity

Artificial satellites

1   What is an artificial satellite?
2   How does an artificial satellite manage to travel from Earth into space?
3   How does an artificial satellite keep in orbit around Earth?
4   Look at the photograph of the artificial satellite.
    What is providing the power to keep it moving?
5   Look at the satellite image at the beginning of this topic. It shows a tropical cyclone. Weather satellites track weather such as cyclones and send photographs to scientists on Earth.
    Why do you think it is useful to see these photographs?
6   Do some research. Find an example of another Earth feature that satellites can photograph and send back to scientists on Earth.
    Share what you have found out with the class.

Have I changed any ideas I used to have about satellites?

Look what I can do!

☐   I can identify the force gravity.
☐   I can use a model to see how a satellite orbits a larger object in space.
☐   I can use a force diagram to show the name and direction of forces acting on an object.
☐   I know that a satellite is an object in space that orbits a larger object.

> 5.3 Friction, air resistance, water resistance and upthrust

We are going to:

- identify upthrust, friction, air resistance and water resistance
- see that an object may have multiple forces acting upon it even when at rest
- use force diagrams to show the name and direction of forces acting on an object
- use knowledge of forces to predict which parachute will fall faster
- describe the accuracy of our prediction, based on results
- decide when measurements need to be repeated to give more reliable data
- measure accurately
- collect and record measurements in a table
- make a parachute and suggest how to improve it
- make a conclusion based on results and knowledge of forces

Getting started

1   Name the two surfaces that rub together as Marcus rides his bike along the path.
2   What is the force between these two surfaces called?
3   What effect does it have on how fast Marcus can ride his bike?
4   Talk about when you are swimming. Is there any friction in the water?

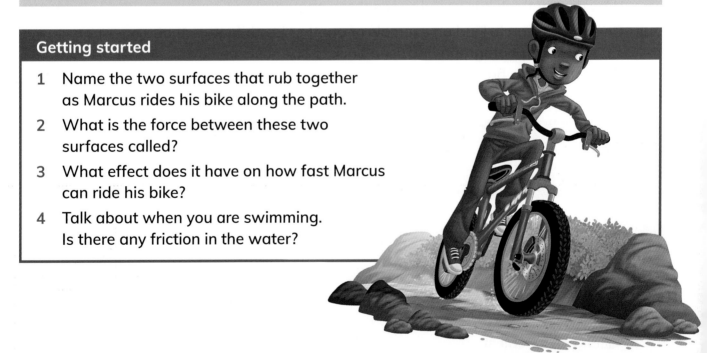

What is friction?

In the picture, Marcus is riding his bike along a gravel path. The bike's tyres and the gravel path try to slide past each other. The force between two surfaces that are trying to slide past each other is called friction. Friction only acts on moving objects. Friction always works in the direction opposite to the direction the object is moving. This slows down the moving object.

Water resistance and air resistance are types of friction. Water resistance is a force that slows things down that are moving through water.

Air resistance is a force that slows things down that are moving through air. Air resistance affects all moving objects on Earth. As objects move, the air pushes against the object, slowing down its movement.

Both water resistance and air resistance are sometimes called drag, because they drag back the moving object.

air resistance	streamlined
drag	upthrust
friction	water resistance

113

Forces in water

Have you tried to push a beach ball down in the sea or a swimming pool? The ball will not stay down. The ball floats on the surface. This is because there is a force in the water that pushes things up. This is called an upthrust force.

Any object that moves through water will be slowed down by the drag or water resistance. The shape of the object can help to reduce the drag. Objects like the fish in the picture have a sleek or streamlined shape. This causes less disturbance of the water and therefore less drag.

Swimmers try to copy the streamlined shape of fish.

Activity

Identify upthrust, gravity and water resistance

Look at the picture of the boat.

1   Identify the force pushing the boat up.
2   Identify the force pushing the boat down.
3   Identify the force that will happen when the boat moves through the water.
4   Draw the boat. Draw and label three arrows to show the forces you identified in questions 1–3.
5   Why do fish move quickly through water?
6   How do we use science to design plastic caps for swimmers?

Air resistance

Air resistance pushes against a moving object, such as a car, and slows it down. The larger the surface area of the moving object, the more air resistance there is.

Air resistance also pushes against falling objects and slows them down. Look at the photograph of hot air balloons. Air resistance helps to keep the balloons up but the people in the basket under the balloon fill the balloon with gas. The gas is lighter than air and the balloon floats.

A parachute uses air resistance to work. The person needs the parachute to help them reach the Earth slowly and safely. It is very light in weight and has a very big surface area. It catches lots of air in it as it falls down. This creates a lot of air resistance.

Think like a scientist

Compare two parachutes

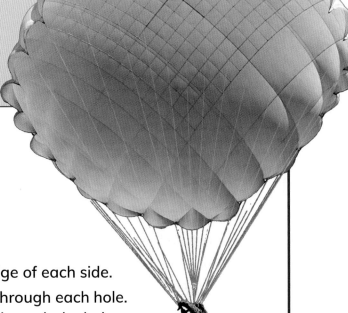

You will need:
thin string, a thin plastic sheet, sticky tape, two identical weights (such as small plastic toys), scissors, a stopwatch

How to make the parachutes

- Cut two squares from the plastic sheet. One square must be 10 × 10 cm and the other square 20 × 20 cm.
- Trim the edges with the scissors to make an eight-sided shape.
- Make a small hole with a pencil near the edge of each side.
- Thread a piece of string about 10 cm long through each hole. Tie knots so that the string does not come through the holes. The strings must be the same length.
- Join the ends of the eight strings with a knot. Attach the object you are using for a weight to the knot with sticky tape.

Continued

Test your parachutes

- Stand on a chair and raise your arm to drop your small parachute. Remember that you want to drop it as slowly as possible, so don't throw it!

Be careful when standing on the chairs - you don't want to fall off!

- Use the stopwatch to record how many seconds it takes for the parachute to reach the ground.

- Repeat three times to check your results.

- Decide whether you need to repeat more times to get more reliable data.

- Record your results in a table.

- Predict whether the larger parachute will fall faster or slower than the small parachute.

- Repeat these steps with the large parachute to test your prediction.

Questions

Answer these questions in your group.

1 Name two forces that acted on your parachute after you dropped it.
2 Draw a force diagram to show the forces acting on your parachute.
3 Calculate the average time it took your small parachute to fall.
4 Calculate the average time it took your large parachute to fall.
5 Which parachute took longer to fall? Was this what you predicted? Explain why one parachute fell faster than the other.

Continued

Questions

6   Suggest a way to change your parachute to make it fall more slowly.

7   Write a conclusion about the speed the parachute falls compared to the size of the parachute and forces acting on it.

How are we doing?

Answer the following questions about your group.

For each question, choose from one of these faces:

How well did we decide when measurements needed to be repeated to give more accurate data?

How well did we measure time accurately and record measurements?

How well did we use results and their knowledge of forces to make a conclusion?

Did I work well in my group? Could I have made a better contribution?

Look what I can do!

☐   I can identify friction, upthrust, air resistance and water resistance (drag).

☐   I can see that an object may have multiple forces acting upon it even when at rest.

☐   I can use force diagrams to show the name and direction of forces acting on an object.

☐   I can use knowledge of forces to predict which parachute will fall faster.

☐   I can describe the accuracy of my prediction, based on results.

☐   I can decide when measurements need to be repeated to give more reliable data.

☐   I can measure accurately.

☐   I can collect and record measurements in a table.

☐   I can make a parachute and suggest how to improve.

☐   I can make a conclusion based on results and knowledge of forces.

> 5.4 Multiple forces

We are going to:

- identify gravity, applied forces, normal forces, upthrust, friction, air resistance and water resistance

- see that an object may have multiple forces acting on it at rest

- make and test a paper aeroplane to demonstrate the forces on it at rest and when it is flying

- use force diagrams to show the name and direction of forces acting on an object, in movement or at rest

- make predictions using knowledge of forces

- describe the accuracy of our predictions, based on results

- suggest how a paper aeroplane could be improved and explain any changes we could make

- make a conclusion from results using our knowledge of forces

multiple

thrust

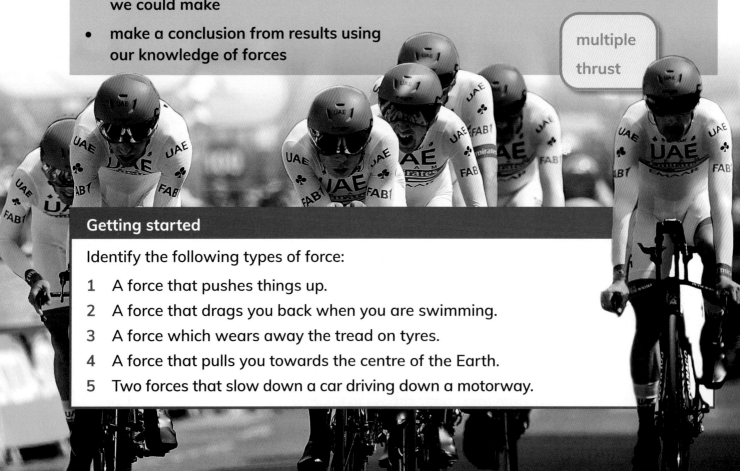

Getting started

Identify the following types of force:

1 A force that pushes things up.
2 A force that drags you back when you are swimming.
3 A force which wears away the tread on tyres.
4 A force that pulls you towards the centre of the Earth.
5 Two forces that slow down a car driving down a motorway.

Many forces act together

All objects are affected by several different forces or **multiple** forces at once. The force that is the strongest will cause the change of an object. The change might be a change of shape, a change of position or a change in the speed an object is travelling.

Look at this example of Sofia rolling a ball.

There are several forces acting on the ball:

- Applied force, as Sofia pushes the ball.
- Gravity pulls the ball down towards the Earth.
- Air resistance slows the ball down once it is moving.
- Friction with the floor slows the ball down once it is moving.

Which forces are acting when you ride a bicycle?

Look at the picture of Marcus riding the bicycle.

Gravity is pulling Marcus and the bicycle towards the centre of the Earth.

Friction between the tyres and the road is pulling him back.

Air resistance is also pulling him back.

To overcome the air resistance and friction Marcus must push on the pedals to push the bicycle forwards. This is **thrust**. Thrust is an applied force.

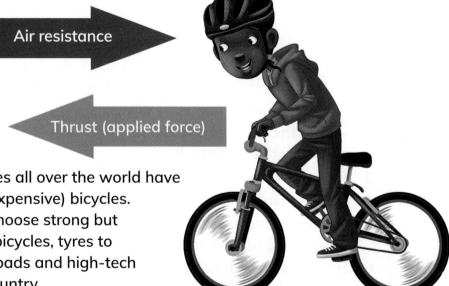

Professional cyclists who enter races all over the world have very carefully designed (and very expensive) bicycles. Designers use science when they choose strong but lightweight materials to make the bicycles, tyres to cope with rough roads or smooth roads and high-tech gears to cope with mountainous country.

Activity

Forces at work when you cycle

1 List four forces involved when you ride a bicycle.
2 Which force is a force applied when you cycle?
3 Look at the photograph of cyclists racing at the start of this topic.
   List the ways these cyclists overcome air resistance.
4 Why is it difficult to cycle on a day when the wind is blowing into your face?
5 Why do cyclists with smooth tyres on a smooth road travel faster?
6 Draw a force diagram to show the five forces acting on the ball that
   Sofia rolls in the picture. (You don't have to draw Sofia, just the ball
   on the floor!)

Forces acting on aeroplanes

Air resistance and gravity are the two forces which act on anything lifted from
the Earth and moved through the air. To overcome these forces we have to
create our own forces of thrust and lifting up. An aeroplane is a good example
of these forces. An aeroplane uses its wings and engines to lift it off the ground
and thrust it forward. You can demonstrate this in the next activity.

Think like a scientist

Make and test a paper aeroplane

You will need:
a sheet of A4 paper

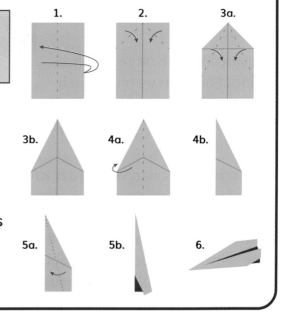

1 Fold the paper in half vertically.
2 Unfold the paper and fold each of the top
   corners into the centre line.
3 Fold the top edges into the centre line.
4 Fold the plane in half toward you.
5 Fold the wings down, matching the top edges
   up with the bottom edge of the body.
6 Hold your aeroplane under the wings and
   launch it into the air.

Continued

Questions

1 While your aeroplane is at rest, what forces are acting on it?

2 Predict what will happen to your aeroplane when you throw it up into the air.

3 Throw your aeroplane upwards and outwards into the air. When you did this, which two natural forces were acting on it?

4 When you threw your aeroplane into the air, what applied forces did you create to overcome the forces you named in question 3?

5 Your paper aeroplane is flying. Copy the diagram of the paper aeroplane. Name each of the four forces marked with arrows.

6 What happened to your aeroplane when you threw it up into the air? Is this what you predicted?

7 Discuss why the aeroplane crashed to the ground.

8 Suggest some changes to make your aeroplane stay up in the air for longer.

9 Discuss how a pilot prevents a real aeroplane from falling to the ground.

10 Write a conclusion about how aeroplanes can overcome forces and fly.

How am I doing?

Can I identify forces on a force diagram of a paper aeroplane?

Can I draw a force diagram much easier than before?

Do I still need more practice?

How did making and testing a paper aeroplane help you to understand multiple forces better?

Look what I can do!

☐ I can identify gravity, normal force, applied forces, friction, thrust, upthrust (lift) and air resistance (drag).

☐ I can make and test a paper aeroplane to demonstrate forces on it at rest and when it is flying.

☐ I can identify the name and direction of forces acting on an object on a force diagram.

☐ I can make predictions using knowledge of forces.

☐ I can describe the accuracy of my predictions based on results.

☐ I can suggest changes to my aeroplane to make it stay in the air for longer.

☐ I can make a conclusion about how aeroplanes are designed to overcome forces.

> 5.5 Magnets and magnetic materials

We are going to:

- find out the difference between a magnet and a magnetic material.

- make predictions about which materials are magnetic and which are not

- plan a fair test to classify materials as magnetic or non-magnetic

- describe how accurate our predictions were

- record results in a table

- describe patterns in results and point out results that do not fit the pattern

- make a conclusion from results

> alloy
>
> magnetic materials

Getting started

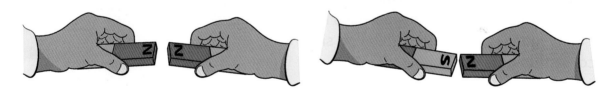

1 What type of magnets are in the pictures?

2 What do the 'N' and 'S' on the magnets show?

3 Complete these sentences about what is shown in the pictures:

When two like poles come close to each other the magnets _____ each other.

When two unlike poles come close to each other the magnets _____ each other.

4 Which of the following materials is magnetic?

wood   iron   glass   plastic   copper

What are magnetic materials?

Magnetic materials are materials that are attracted to a magnet. Fridge magnets stick to a fridge because the fridge is made from a magnetic material.

You already know that some metal objects are attracted to a magnet but non-metals like plastic and wood are not attracted to a magnet.

Which metals are magnetic?

Some metals are precious, such as silver, gold and platinum. None of these metals is magnetic. Some of the metals that we use in everyday life are iron, steel, aluminium, copper and chromium. Often things are made from a mixture of metals. A mixture of metals is called an **alloy**. For example, steel is an alloy made mainly from iron. It is much stronger than iron. We use steel to make machines, steel pipes and bridges.

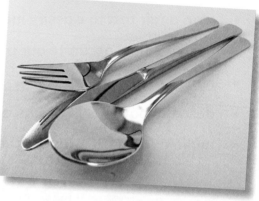

Chromium is mixed with steel to make an alloy called stainless steel. Stainless steel does not rust. It is used in many objects such as knives, sinks and medical instruments.

Brass is an alloy of copper and zinc. We use brass to make door handles and ornaments.

If you hold a magnet next to an object and you can feel the pulling force of the magnet, the object is attracted to the magnet. This means the object is made of magnetic material. You are going to test some metals and alloys to see if they are magnetic or not. Remember that if the object is made from an alloy you will be testing more than one metal at the same time.

Think like a scientist

Test metals to classify metals and alloys as magnetic or non-magnetic

You will need:
a magnet; a selection of things made from different metals and alloys, such as steel wool, a copper scourer, copper wires, a brass handle or brass candle stick, steel pins, steel screws, stainless steel cutlery, steel paperclips (no plastic covering), an iron bolt or nail, copper and nickel coins, aluminium foil, a cast iron cooking pot.

- List the objects you have chosen and identify the metal or alloy that each object is made from.
- Copy the table and fill in the first two columns.

Object	Metal or alloy object is made from	Prediction: magnetic or not?	Result: magnetic or not?

- Predict which objects will be magnetic. Fill in the third column of your table.
- Plan a fair test to test your prediction.
- Tick the final column if the object is magnetic.

Questions

1 How well did your results match your predictions?

2 Describe a pattern in your results. Was there a metal or alloy that did not fit the pattern which you were surprised about?

3 Write a conclusion about which metals are magnetic and which are non-magnetic.

4 List two ways that your test was a fair test.

5 Which types of scientific enquiry did you practice in this activity?

6 Choose two objects that you have found to be made of magnetic material. Hold them close together. Are they attracted to one another?

Continued

How am I doing?

Am I getting better at fair testing, describing a pattern in results and writing a conclusion based on my science knowledge?

Rate yourself with ticks: ✓ or ✓✓ or ✓✓✓

What is the difference between a magnet and a magnetic material?

A magnet is a material that has an area around it where magnetic force is active. We can't see this area. In this area a magnet can attract or repel other magnets and it can attract a magnetic material.

A magnetic material does not have an area around it where magnetic force is active, like a magnet does. So a magnetic material cannot attract another magnetic material, as you discovered in question 5 in the Think like a scientist investigation. A magnetic material can only be attracted to a magnet when it is in the magnet's area of magnetic force.

Industry can use the fact that a magnet attracts magnetic materials. This photograph shows a very strong magnet in use in a scrap yard. The magnet attracts the steel parts of the cars and leaves behind the plastic and glass.

Activity

Magnets and magnetic materials

1 a Name two magnetic metals.

   b How can you test they are magnetic?

2 a Name two non-magnetic metals.

   b How can you test they are non-magnetic?

   c Are the two non-magnetic metals you chose attracted to each other? Explain why or why not.

3 Name a non-magnetic alloy.

Continued

4   Do you have a magnet at home, such as a fridge magnet?
    Use your magnet to carry out these tests:

   a   Find at least three examples of objects you use at home that are
        made of metals. Which metals are they made from?

   b   Use your magnet to test whether these objects are magnetic or not.

   c   Record your information in a table.

5   Suggest how magnets can be used for sorting used steel cans and aluminium
    cans so that they can be recycled separately.

How am I doing?

Do I understand the difference between a magnet and a magnetic material?

Choose from one of these faces: or or 🙁

How can you use the knowledge you have gained from this topic?

Look what I can do!

☐   I can understand the difference between a magnet and a magnetic material.

☐   I can make predictions about which materials are magnetic and
    which are not.

☐   I can plan and carry out a fair test.

☐   I can describe how accurate my predictions were.

☐   I can classify objects as magnetic or non-magnetic through testing.

☐   I can record results in a table.

☐   I can describe patterns in results and see that sometimes a result
    does not fit the pattern.

☐   I can make a conclusion from results.

> 5.6 Magnetic force

We are going to:

- see that forces act over a distance between magnets, and between a magnet and a magnetic material

- know that magnets can have different magnetic strengths

- plan a fair test and identify the independent, dependent and control variables

- take accurate measurements

- decide when to repeat measurements to get more reliable data

- record results in a table

- present and interpret results in a bar chart

- make a conclusion from results

Getting started

What is the difference between a magnet and a magnetic material? Complete these sentences for your answer.

A magnet is a material that has an area around it where _____ is active.

In this area a magnet can attract or _____ other _____ and it can attract a _____ material.

A magnetic material does _____ have an area around it where magnetic force is active. So a magnetic material cannot _____ another magnetic material.

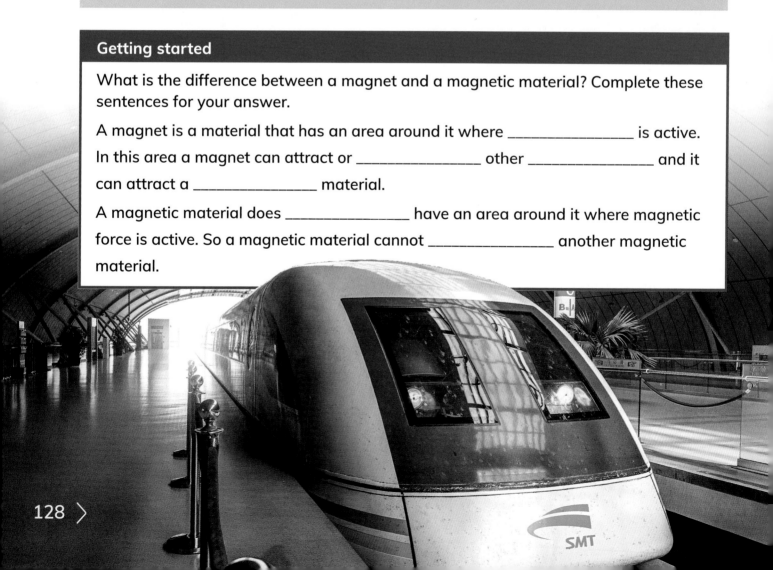

Forces between magnets

Arun is holding two magnets so that they can swing freely. If the unlike poles are facing one another, the magnets are attracted to each other. This shows the magnetic force of attraction between them. Arun finds that the magnets are attracted to each other when they are still a distance apart. This shows that the force between magnets can act over a distance.

Remember that a magnet is a material that has an area around it where magnetic force is active. So as long as Arun holds the second magnet inside this area the two magnets will be attracted to one another. The stronger the magnets, the bigger the area and the bigger the distance can be.

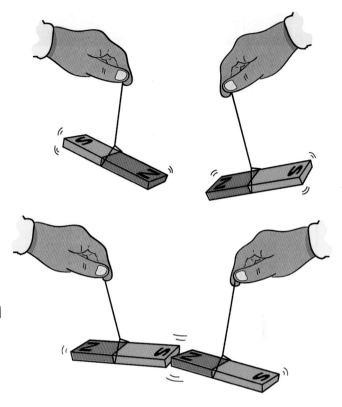

Strength of magnets

Magnets can be extremely strong. Look at the Maglev train in the photograph at the start of this topic. This high-speed train uses magnets to work! Scientists have used their knowledge of magnets to invent tracks that are made of very strong magnets. The train floats above the tracks.

We will work with much weaker magnets in class! Let's investigate how far apart a magnet and a magnetic material can be for the magnetic material to be attracted to the magnet. We are going to compare different poles of two magnets to see if some magnets or poles of magnets are stronger than others.

Think like a scientist

Test the strength of magnets

You will need:
two different magnets, such as a bar magnet and a horseshoe magnet;
a metal paperclip with no plastic coating; a 30 cm plastic or wooden ruler

- Draw a table to record your results in:

Magnet	Distance in mm – first reading	Distance in mm – second reading	Distance in mm – third reading	Average (mean) reading in mm
Magnet 1 – N pole				
Magnet 1 – S pole				
Magnet 2 – N pole				
Magnet 2 – S pole				

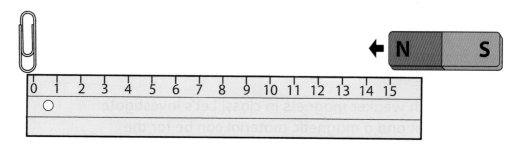

- Your ruler remains in the same position during the activity.
- Place the paperclip at the '0' end of your ruler. The position of the paperclip is dependent on changes of the magnet. We are going to measure these changes.
- Place the north pole of Magnet 1 at the other end of your ruler. You are going to change the magnet during the activity.

Continued

- Slowly move your magnet towards the paperclip.

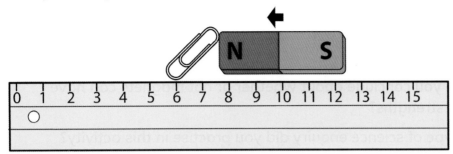

- Stop the magnet as soon as the paperclip is attracted to and touches the magnet. Read off the distance in millimetres on the ruler. Record the distance on your table. This is the first reading.
- Repeat to find a second and third reading for the north pole of Magnet 1.
- Carry out the activity again with the south pole of Magnet 1. Fill in the table.
- Repeat the activity to test the strength of your other magnet.
- Calculate the mean readings and fill in the mean reading column of the table. To calculate the mean reading, add together the three readings and divide the sum by three. For example, if your three readings were 3.2 mm, 3.4 mm and 3.0 mm the sum is 9.6 mm and the mean reading is 9.6 mm ÷ 3 = 3.2 mm.
- Draw a bar chart to present your results. Use the mean readings. Use a scale of 1 cm represents 5 mm. Draw a bar for each pole of each magnet. Give your graph a suitable heading.

Questions

1 Why can't you use a steel ruler for this activity?

2 Why did you use a steel paperclip?

3 How did this activity show that forces between a magnet and a magnetic material act over a distance?

4 Were the three measurements for each magnet always the same?

5 Why is it good scientific practice to take each measurement more than once?

6 Were the strengths of the north and south poles of each magnet different or the same?

7 What did you do to make sure your test was fair?

Continued

8   Identify the control variable and the dependent and independent variables.

9   Why did one of the magnets attract the paperclip from a greater distance away?

10 What do you conclude about whether or not magnets can have different strengths?

11 Which type of science enquiry did you practise in this activity?

How am I doing?

Answer 'easily', 'not sure' or 'no, I am not able to do this yet' to the following question:

Can I identify the control, dependent and independent variables in an investigation?

Did your group repeat measurements enough to get accurate results?

Look what I can do!

☐   I can see that forces act over a distance between magnets, and between a magnet and a magnetic material.

☐   I can see that magnets have different strengths.

☐   I can plan and carry out a fair test to find out if magnets have different magnetic strengths and identify the independent, dependent and control variables.

☐   I can measure distances accurately.

☐   I can repeat measurements to give more reliable data.

☐   I can record measurements in a table.

☐   I can present results in a bar chart.

☐   I can make a conclusion from results.

Project: How people use forces in my area

In this project you are going to use your knowledge of forces to describe how forces are used in a machine or equipment.

Choose a business, factory, transport or farm to visit in your area that uses a machine or equipment where you can identify the forces.

Here are some examples:

- farm equipment such as a pump or a tractor
- a sewing factory that makes clothes
- a factory that makes car parts or computers or any household appliance
- a bus or train service
- a scrapyard that uses magnets to separate iron and steel from other metals
- a water-purification centre.

Work in pairs or small groups. Decide what you will choose for your project. Ask your teacher if they think this is suitable.

Make a questionnaire with questions to ask on your visit. Questions can include:

- What machines do you use?
- How does the machine operate? Does it use electricity or fuel?
- What slows down the machine? Is there friction with air or water, or between surfaces?
- How can you overcome the friction?

Visit your chosen example. Go with an adult or older brother or sister. Take your questionnaire and a pencil and notebook. Take photographs if possible (ask permission first!). Or make drawings.

Make a simple force diagram of the machine or equipment you see.

Arrange your pictures and information on an A4 sheet of paper.

Give your project a heading.

Check your progress

1   Match each word from 1 to 5 with its meaning A to E.

Word	Meaning
1 Gravity	A: A mixture of metals
2 Magnetic material	B: A body in space which moves around a larger body in space
3 Applied force	C: A material that is attracted to a magnet
4 Alloy	D: A force which attracts all objects towards the Earth
5 Satellite	E: A force that is applied to another object or person

2   Identify the type of force acting in each of these pictures.

A   B   C   D

3   Which of the following materials are magnetic and which are non-magnetic?

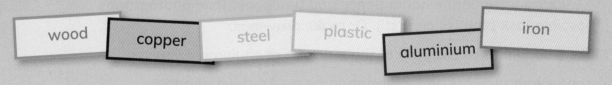

wood   copper   steel   plastic   aluminium   iron

Continued

4 a Copy this picture of a submarine.

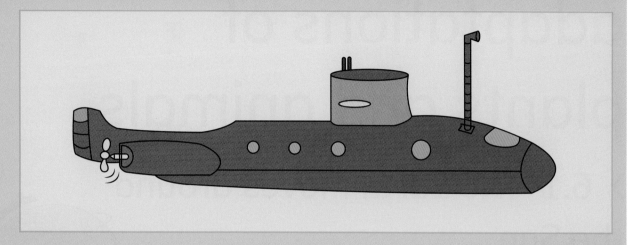

   b On your picture label the four forces which act on the submarine when it is moving through the water. Show the direction and name of each force.

   c When the submarine is at rest, which two forces are acting on it?

   d What causes the thrust?

   e Describe the submarine's shape.

   f Why does a submarine have this shape?

5 Arun and Marcus are comparing the strength of two magnets.
   They are using a plastic ruler and a steel drawing pin.

   a Why are Arun and Marcus using a steel drawing pin?

   b Why are they using a plastic ruler?

   c What is the control variable in their investigation?

   d What is the dependent variable?

   e What is the independent variable?

   f How does their investigation show which magnet is the strongest?

6 Seasons and adaptations of plants and animals

> 6.1 The Earth moves around the Sun

We are going to:

- describe the orbit of the Earth around the Sun

- describe how the tilt of the Earth can create different seasons in different places

- use diagrams as models to describe the Earth's orbit around the Sun and seasons

- know that a diagram can show some of the important features

- use the internet and library books to answer questions

Getting started

1   What is this model of the Earth called?

2   What does the stick through the Earth represent?

3   What causes day and night?

Earth's orbit

As well as turning on its axis, the Earth revolves, or moves around, the Sun.

The path the Earth travels in around the Sun is called an orbit.

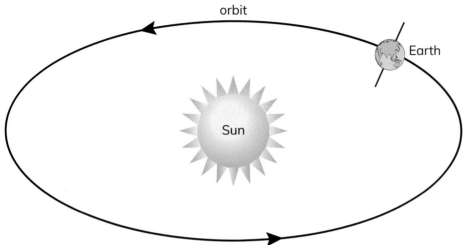

ellipse

hemisphere

North Pole

orbit

revolve

season

slight ellipse

South Pole

tilt

year

The orbit is shaped a bit like an egg. This shape is called an ellipse. The orbit is not a perfect ellipse so scientists call it a slight ellipse.

Because of the shape of the orbit, the Earth is sometimes closer to the Sun and sometimes further away from the Sun. The average distance between the Earth and the Sun is 150 million km.

The Earth moves around the Sun in an anticlockwise direction.

It takes 365¼ days or 1 year for the Earth to complete its orbit around the Sun. In that time the Earth has travelled 940 million km!

The Sun is bigger than the Earth. So the Sun exerts a bigger gravitational force on the Earth than the Earth does on the Sun.

Think like a scientist

A model of Earth's orbit

1   Give reasons why the diagram above is a good model of the Earth orbiting the Sun.

2   In what way is the diagram not a good model?

3   Why is the shape of the orbit described as a 'slight ellipse'?

4   Which force keeps the Earth in its orbit around the Sun?

Continued

5   While the Earth is orbiting the Sun, what other movement is the Earth making?

6   One year is 365¼ days. But we don't have one day in the year that is only 6 hours long. How do we manage the ¼ day? (Use the internet to find this answer.)

The seasons

The seasons are spring, summer, autumn and winter. Seasons are caused by the Earth orbiting the sun once a year and the tilt of the Earth's axis. Each season occurs when the Earth is at a particular position in its orbit around the Sun.

The months that you experience each season depend on which hemisphere you live in. Countries between the Equator and the North Pole are in the northern hemisphere. Countries between the Equator and the South Pole are in the southern hemisphere.

When the northern hemisphere has summer, the southern hemisphere has winter. This is because the northern hemisphere is tilted towards the Sun. In summer the days are long and the nights are short. At the Equator there are no distinct seasons – there is equal day and night on every day of the year.

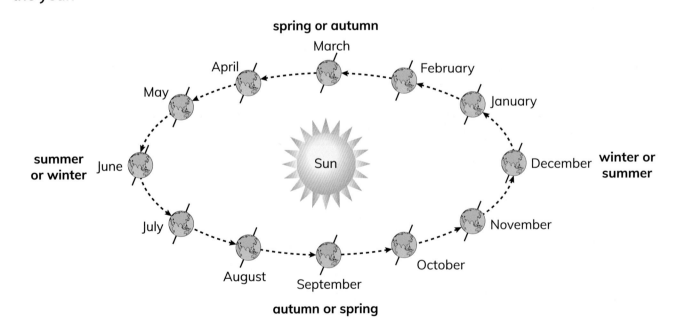

Look at the diagram of the positions of Earth each month in its orbit around the Sun.

Find Earth in the June position. Because of the tilted axis, notice that the northern hemisphere is tilted towards the Sun. This means the northern hemisphere is having more daylight than darkness. The northern hemisphere is having summer. The southern hemisphere is tilted away from the Sun and is therefore having winter.

Now find the Earth in the March position. Notice that the whole Earth is facing the Sun. As the Earth rotates on its axis all the Earth will be facing away from the Sun. Both hemispheres are having an equal amount of day and night. March is autumn in the southern hemisphere and spring in the northern hemisphere.

Activity 1

Find information on a diagram of Earth in its orbit

On the diagram of the seasons, find Earth in the December position in its orbit.

1 Which hemisphere is tilted towards the Sun?
2 Which hemisphere is having summer? Why?

Find the September position of the Earth in its orbit.

3 Which hemisphere is tilted towards the Sun?
4 Which season is the northern hemisphere having?
5 Which season is the southern hemisphere having?
6 Which two factors cause the seasons?

How am I doing?

How well can I get information about seasons from a diagram of the Earth in its orbit around the Sun? Choose one from:

- Very well.
- Only sometimes.
- I need some help with this.

Different seasons in different parts of the world

Look at the diagram below which shows the Earth in its December position in its orbit around the Sun.

Notice that:

- the side of Earth facing the Sun is having day

- the side of Earth facing away from the Sun is having night

- the tilted axis causes the southern hemisphere to be tilted towards the Sun

- the region around the South Pole is having continuous daylight!

Sun's rays travelling to Earth

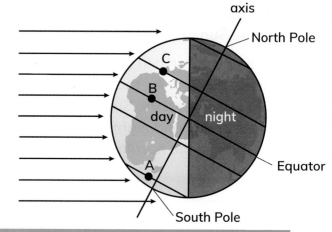

Activity 2

Use a diagram to find information about the seasons

Use the diagram to answer questions 1–3.

1   Which hemisphere is having summer? How do you know this?

2   Which part of the world is having 24 hours of darkness?

3   What is the length of day at each of the points A, B and C?

4   If you lived on the Equator would you have seasons? Explain why or why not.

5   The photograph on the next page shows the midnight Sun. It was taken at midnight in December! In which part of the world do you think this photograph could have been taken?

Do the diagrams in this topic help you to understand how seasons occur?

Look what I can do!

- ☐ I can describe the orbit of the Earth around the Sun.
- ☐ I can describe how the tilt of the Earth creates different seasons in different places.
- ☐ I can use diagrams as models to describe the Earth's orbit around the Sun and seasons.
- ☐ I know that a diagram can show me some of the important features.
- ☐ I can use the internet and library books to answer questions.

> 6.2 Seasonal changes

We are going to:

- describe how the tilt of the Earth can create different seasons in different places

- make predictions about length of day

- describe patterns in data

- present and interpret data on a line graph

- use different sources to find information

- make a conclusion based on scientific understanding

adapt	migration
chlorophyll	sunrise
dormant	sunset
hibernation	

Getting started

1 This a picture of the sunrise. In which direction does the Sun appear to rise?

2 What does the Sun appear to do during the day?

3 What does the Sun appear to do in the evening?

4 Does the Sun really move across the sky?
   Explain what causes day and night.

5 Which months are summer months in your country?

6 Talk about what you notice when summer turns into autumn.

Sunrise and sunset times

Do you think the Sun rises and sets at the same time every day of the year?
Let's investigate.

Think like a scientist

Record and present length of day data

Look at the times of sunrise and sunset for Cape Town during a week
in February and a week in March. The length of day is calculated
by subtracting the sunrise time from the sunset time.

Sunrise and sunset times for Cape Town, South Africa

Date	Sunrise	Sunset	Length of day
1 February	06:08	19:51	13h 43m
2 February	06:09	19:51	13h 42m
3 February	06:10	19:50	13h 40m
4 February	06:11	19:49	13h 38m
5 February	06:12	19:48	13h 36m
6 February	06:13	19:47	13h 34m
7 February	06:14	19:46	13h 32m
14 March	06:45	19:06	12h 21m
15 March	06:46	19:04	12h 18m
16 March	06:46	19:03	12h 17m
17 March	06:47	19:01	12h 14m
18 March	06:48	19:00	12h 12m
19 March	06:49	18:59	12h 10m
20 March	06:50	18:57	12h 07m

Continued

1 Work out the difference in the lengths of day between 3 February and 7 February. Repeat these calculations for the period between 16 March and 20 March. Between 3 February and 20 March are the days in Cape Town getting longer or shorter?

2 a Which season is Cape Town having in February?

   b Which season is Cape Town having in March?

3 a Predict how the length of day will change during the month of April.

   b How could you test your prediction?

4 Explain why, using knowledge from the last topic, the length of day changes.

5 Collect data for sunrise and sunset times for a week where you live.

6 Present the data in a table. Draw line graphs to show your data. You can look at the instructions in the 'New science skills' section at the end of this book to see how to draw a line graph.

7 Compare the pattern of changing length of day in Cape Town in the months of February and March with the pattern of changing length of day during the same months where you live.

8 Write a conclusion about the changes in the length of day throughout a year.

As humans, we wear different clothes in summer and winter and heat our home if the winter is cold – we adapt to the changing weather. But how are plants and animals adapted to the seasons?

How plants are adapted to the seasons

Look at the photograph at the start of the unit. It shows trees in Srinigar, Kashmir, during autumn. In many parts of the world, autumn is the season when leaves change from green to yellow and red.

Plant leaves are green because they contain a green substance called chlorophyll. The chlorophyll in the leaves helps to produce food for the tree. During autumn, days become shorter and there is less sunlight. The leaves are no longer able to produce food for the tree.

The chlorophyll begins to break down, leaving the leaves yellow and red and then brown. After a few weeks the leaves fall off the tree.

During the cold winter months the tree has no leaves at all. It is dormant or sleeping. In spring, when the days begin to warm up, we see new leaf buds on the branches. By summer the trees are covered in green leaves again.

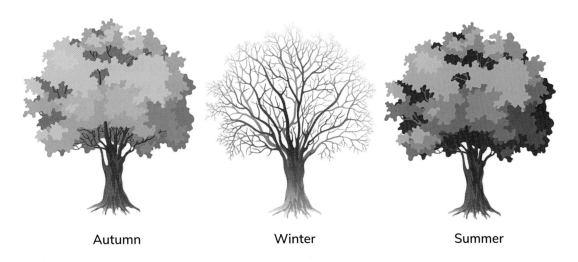

| Autumn | Winter | Summer |

Activity 1

How plants are adapted to the seasons

Look at the photograph of trees in Srinigar, Kashmir, shown at the start of this unit.

1   How does the photograph show that the season is autumn?

2   What will happen to the leaves during the next season?

3   Copy and complete this sentence to explain why the trees change.

During autumn, days become _____. Leaves are no longer able to produce _____ because there is not enough _____.
The _____ change colour and then _____ off.

4   Why do you think people in the USA call autumn 'fall'?

5   Give examples of trees that change colour in your country.
    You may need to do some research to find the answer.

How animals are adapted to the seasons

Some animals cannot find food to eat during the winter. These animals have two choices to stay alive: stay where they are and hibernate or migrate to a warmer region.

Hibernation

Hibernation describes how the animal's body goes into a dormant state for a long period of time. When an animal hibernates, its heart rate and breathing slow down, and its temperature goes down . At the end of autumn the days are getting shorter and colder. Animals like bears eat a lot of food to give them an extra layer of fat to help them survive the long, cold winter. Other animals, like mice, collect a pile of nuts and seeds to last them through the winter. They find an underground home for the winter and go into a dormant state. When spring arrives the animals become active again.

Migration

When seasons change and there is no longer enough food to eat, some animals migrate to warmer regions where there is food.

Animals that eat grass need a supply of grass all year round. But in many parts of the world the grass dries up in the hot dry summer. The animals have to walk long distances to a region where there is new grass to eat. This is called a migration. Look at the photograph here. It shows wildebeest (also called gnu), in central Africa. Two million wildebeest migrate 3000 km every year to find food. Their migration depends on the seasons and where the rains are. They know that the rains will bring new grass.

Many different types of birds migrate. In late summer, as the days get shorter, many birds begin their migration. They eat more food so that they will have the strength to survive the long journey. Then huge numbers of them fly long distances to a place where there is food for them.

For example, Siberian cranes migrate from Russia and northern Europe to India. They leave at the end of summer and fly south to India where it is warm and they can find food.

Activity 2

How animals are adapted to changes in seasons

1 a What is hibernation?

   b Give an example of an animal that hibernates in your country.

2 Read this story about whale migration, then answer the questions below.

> Grey whales spend the summer in the cold waters of the Arctic Ocean. There
> is plenty of food for them so they increase their weight by about one-third.
> In winter the water freezes in the Arctic Ocean. The whales migrate south
> to the Pacific Ocean off the coast of Mexico. They swim 8000 km in two
> months! In the warm water the whales have their babies. In spring they
> swim 8000 km back to the Arctic to feed during the summer.

   a Why do grey whales migrate to the Arctic Ocean?

   b Why do they have to leave the Arctic Ocean in winter?

   c Why do the grey whales swim to the Pacific Ocean off the coast of Mexico?

   d When do the grey whales return to the Arctic Ocean?

3 a Work with a partner. Choose a bird that migrates to your country.

   b Do some research. Name the bird, find pictures of it and
      describe the journey it makes when it migrates.

   c Present your information to the class.

How am I doing?

How well can I find information by reading a story?

Rate yourself with one of these faces:

How did analysing the length of day data help
me to understand seasonal changes?

Look what I can do!

- ☐ I can make predictions about length of day.
- ☐ I can describe patterns in data.
- ☐ I can present data on a line graph.
- ☐ I can make a conclusion based on scientific understanding.
- ☐ I can describe how the tilt of the Earth can create different seasons in different places.
- ☐ I can use different sources to find information to answer questions.

> 6.3 Plants and animals are adapted to different environments

We are going to:

- describe how plants and animals are adapted to hot, wet, cold or dry environments

- use secondary information sources to research questions

- group plants and animals with environments they are adapted to

Getting started

Look at the photographs.

1 Which photograph do you think shows a hot, wet environment? Why?

2 Which photograph do you think shows a cold environment? Why?

3 Talk about which animals you think might live in the region shown in each picture.

4 Suggest what these animals might eat.

A   B

Adaptations of plants and animals in hot, dry environments

Adaptations are features that help plants and animals to live in their environments.

In a hot, dry environment there is very little water. The small amount of rain dries up quickly because of the heat. Plants and animals are adapted to these conditions by using very little water. The cactus plant and the camel are both good examples.

adaptation
burrow
fin
gills
gland
resin
thaw
thorn
waxy

Thorns instead of leaves allow it to lose less water

Waxy coating stops water from escaping

Fat stem to store water

Deep roots to find water

Long eyelashes to keep sand out of eyes

Thick lips so they can eat thorny desert plants

Camels can survive for a week or more without water and several months with no food. Humps store fat for energy

Wide tough feet so they can walk on hot sand more easily

Smaller animals like rats and lizards also live in hot dry places. They dig **burrows** to stay in during the hot days. They only come out of their burrows at night when it is cooler.

Activity 1

How plants and animals are adapted to hot, dry environments

1   Copy and complete these sentences.
    In a hot, dry environment:
    a   plants have _____ instead of leaves.
    b   roots go _____ under the surface to find _____ .
    c   plants store water in fat _____ .
    d   plants have _____ coatings to prevent water loss.
    e   plant-eating animals must be able to eat _____ plants.
    f   small animals dig _____ to keep cool during the hot days.
    g   animals must be able to survive without much _____ .
2   Work with a partner. Think of other animals that live in hot, dry places. Share your ideas with the class.

How am I doing?

How well can I get information from pictures? Rate yourself with a ★★★ or ★★ or ★

Adaptations of plants and animals in wet environments

Water lilies and lotus plants live in water. They have adaptations such as:

- Large flat leaves which float on the water.

- Big air spaces in the leaves and stems so they can float and leaves can absorb sunlight at the water surface.

- Weak stems because the water supports the plant.

- Small roots because the plant is in water all the time and doesn't need to be anchored in the soil.

Fish are adapted to their environment because they have gills. Gills allow fish to absorb oxygen from the water. Fins allow the fish to move through the water.

Many birds, such as ducks and geese, swim in water. They have webbed feet to help them to do this. This is like wearing flippers when you go swimming!

Seabirds have waterproof feathers so that they can dive for food. Seabirds also have special glands that get rid of salt that they take in when they drink seawater.

Flamingoes live in a shallow water environment. Their long, thin legs allow them to walk through water easily. Their long flexible necks allow them to reach food below the water surface.

Think like a scientist

Research plants and animals that live in a wet environment

- Work with a partner.
- Choose a plant and an animal that live in a wet environment in your country. It can be a freshwater environment like a river or a lake or it can be the sea.
- Name the plant and animal.
- Find pictures of the plant and animal.
- Describe the environment the plant and animal live in.
- List all the ways in which your plant and animal are adapted to their environment.
- Present your findings in class.

How are we doing?

How well did you and your partner:

- share ideas?
- collect information?
- encourage each other?
- present your work?

Give yourselves ★ ★ ★ or ★ ★ or ★ for each of these questions.

Adaptations of plants and animals in cold environments

There are very cold environments in the far north and the far south of the world. Remember these are the regions that have long summer days but also very long dark winters. There is not much rain but there is a lot of snow in winter.

Some animals have thick fur to keep them warm. But during the winter, when there is no food, some animals either hibernate or migrate.

The soil in cold regions freezes in winter. In summer the top few centimetres thaw. Trees and other plants have adaptations for these conditions. For example, trees have resin on their bark. This is a sticky substance that helps to keep the tree warm and prevents the tree from losing moisture.

Activity 2

How plants and animals are adapted to a cold, dry environment

| brown bear | moose | squirrel | fir tree |

1   Match the adaptations (1–4) of the tree in the picture with the reasons for these adaptations (A–D).

Adaptation	Reason
1 Shallow roots	A Snow can slide off the branches
2 Needles with waxy surface	B Prevents too much water loss
3 Sloping branches	C Keeps tree trunk warm and prevents water loss
4 Thick bark and resin	D Tree grows in soil that will not be frozen in summer

2   Which animals in the pictures do you think will hibernate in the winter?

3   Which animal in the pictures do you think will migrate in the winter?

Did I do my best in the research activity?

Look what I can do!

☐   I can describe how plants and animals are adapted to hot, wet, cold or dry environments.

☐   I can use secondary information sources to research questions.

☐   I can group plants and animals according to the environments they are adapted to.

> 6.4 Adaptations of predators and prey

Getting started

Match the predators with their prey in the pictures.

lizard   fly   hawk (bird of prey)

antelope (springbok)   polar bear

seal   spider   cheetah

Predators and prey

A cheetah has adaptations which make it a very successful predator:

- A cheetah can run at 112 km/h – more than four times faster than a human running at top speed. A cheetah has a streamlined shape to help it to run this fast.
- Its eyes are in the front of its head so that the cheetah can judge distance well.
- When the cheetah is crouched low, watching its prey, it is well-camouflaged. This is because its colours blend in with the dry grass environment.

The springbok is the prey. Springbok stay together in large groups. This is their most important adaptation to avoid being caught and eaten. But there is often a springbok that gets left behind the group or which cannot run so fast. These are the animals that the predator hunts and kills.

All predators have adaptations to help them catch their prey. All prey animals have adaptations to avoid being caught.

blend in

camouflage

pack

quills

teamwork

venom

warn

weapon

Adaptations of predators

Examples of adaptations that predators have are:

- speed
- streamlined body shape
- camouflage
- venom

- trapping
- very good eyesight
- a good sense of smell
- sharp powerful teeth

- sharp claws
- teamwork
- a good sense of hearing

Questions

1 Which adaptation from the list on the previous page do you think a spider has to make it a successful predator?

Here are some more examples.

The chameleon can shoot its tongue out so far and so fast that the beetle doesn't stand a chance. Can you spot the chameleon in the right-hand photograph? Chameleons use camouflage to hide from their prey.

Many snakes, like the cobra in the photograph, have venom.
The cobra spits its venom on to its prey to kill it.

2   What other adaptations does the
    snake have that you can see in
    the photograph?

Other snakes bite their prey and inject them
with venom. Other animals, such as scorpions,
also poison their prey with venom.
Eagles have very good eyesight. They can spot
their prey when it is 3 km away! They also have
sharp talons for gripping their prey.

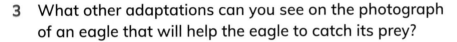

3   What other adaptations can you see on the photograph
    of an eagle that will help the eagle to catch its prey?

Wild hunting dogs hunt in a group or pack. The dogs work in a team to
surround their prey. Dogs and bears also have a very good sense of smell.
They can smell their prey long before they can see it.

4   What other adaptations do the dogs in the photograph have which
    will help them to catch their prey?

5   What adaptations does the crocodile have to catch its prey?

Think like a scientist

Group predators according to their adaptations

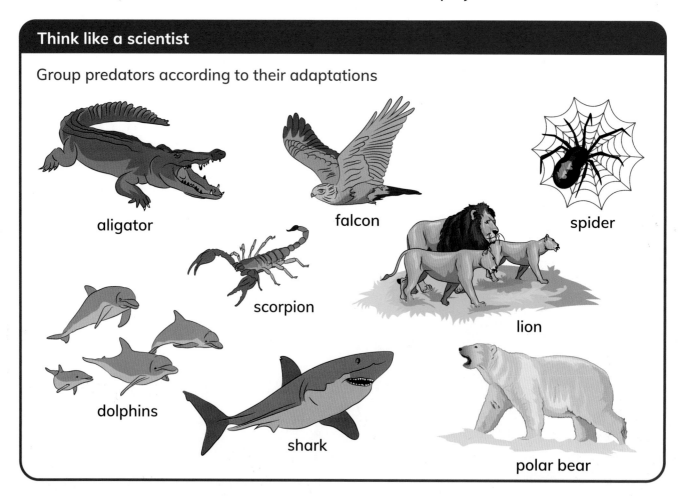

aligator

falcon

spider

scorpion

lion

dolphins

shark

polar bear

Continued

- Work with a partner. Copy the table. Decide what adaptations each of these predators has. Most predators will have several of the adaptations. Tick the correct boxes.

Adaptation	Shark	Falcon	Spider	Dolphin	Scorpion	Polar bear	Alligator	Lion
Teamwork								
Streamlined shape for speed								
Eyes in front of head								
Trapping								
Sharp teeth								
Good eyesight								
Camouflage								
Venom								
Good sense of smell								

- Which scientific enquiry skill did you practise in this activity? If you are not sure refer to the 'Working like a scientist' section at the beginning of this book

- Choose a predator that has not been mentioned in this book. Do some research. List all the adaptations your chosen predator has. Bring your information to share with the class.

How are we doing?

How did you and your partner manage this activity?

How well did you settle disagreements?

Answer 'Well', 'Quite well' or 'Not well' for each question.

Adaptations of prey

Prey animals need to either defend themselves in some way or attack their predator.

Defence – hiding

Hiding from a predator is one way of defence. You saw how a chameleon uses camouflage to blend in with its surroundings so that it can catch its prey. But it also does the same thing to hide from its predators.

Other animals use camouflage to hide. Look how well this moth and this fish blend into their surroundings!

Defence – staying in a group

Many animals stay in a group for safety. The grass-eaters such as zebras, antelopes and wildebeest are prey for predators such as lions and cheetahs. They stay in large groups. Sometimes animals in the group have 'look-out duty' and have to warn the rest of the group with a special sound if they see a predator.

Fish often stay in big groups to defend themselves from bigger fish that eat them. Look at all these sardines defending themselves from dolphins.

Bees live in big groups in a hive. Bees use smell as a signal. If a predator comes close to the bee hive, the guard bees give off a special smell. They beat their wings to spread the smell. Other bees join the guard bees to defend the hive.

Defence – protection

Tortoises and turtles are very slow movers. But they have a hard shell. When a predator approaches they pull their head in under their shell for protection.

Defence – seeing sideways

Many prey animals have eyes at the sides of their heads. This allows them to see a predator on both sides of them. Lizards, antelopes and fish are examples.

Defence – getting away fast

Being fast is a good way to escape from your enemy. For example, antelopes can run fast when a lion or a cheetah is chasing them.

An octopus has eight legs and eyes on each side of its head. When an octopus sees a predator, it shoots out a cloud of ink to confuse it. Then it swims away very fast, leaving its predator surrounded by ink.

Attack

Some prey try to frighten their predators away with weapons such as stings, horns and quills.

Bees and wasps sting the predator. Some ants spray the predator with acid.

Many animals such as rhinos, antelope, gemsbok and buffalos have big, pointed horns. They can use their horns as a weapon if a predator attacks them.

A porcupine spreads out and rattles its quills to make it look and sound more dangerous. If the predator doesn't run away, the porcupine charges backwards and stabs the predator with its quills. The quills often break off, leaving the predator full of painful quills.

Activity

Adaptations of prey

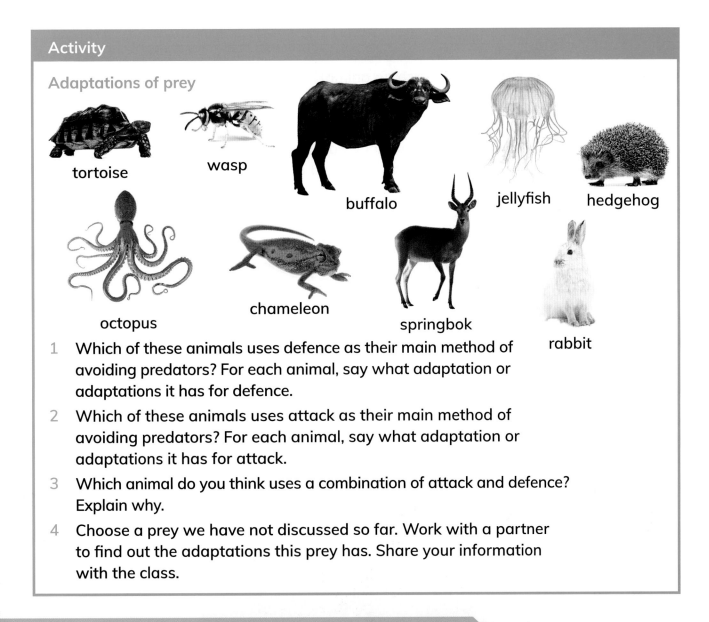

tortoise

wasp

buffalo

jellyfish

hedgehog

octopus

chameleon

springbok

rabbit

1 Which of these animals uses defence as their main method of avoiding predators? For each animal, say what adaptation or adaptations it has for defence.

2 Which of these animals uses attack as their main method of avoiding predators? For each animal, say what adaptation or adaptations it has for attack.

3 Which animal do you think uses a combination of attack and defence? Explain why.

4 Choose a prey we have not discussed so far. Work with a partner to find out the adaptations this prey has. Share your information with the class.

How did the photographs help me to learn about adaptations of predators and prey?

Look what I can do!

☐ I can describe adaptations of predators and prey.

☐ I can use secondary information sources to research questions.

☐ I can group predators and prey according to their adaptations.

Project: Animals at risk

In this project you are going to research an animal in your country which is at risk because people are destroying its environment.

Many animals are at risk because human behaviour and actions are having a negative effect on their environment. For example, plastic pollution is killing seabirds, dolphins and fish. Rapid growth of cites is taking away the environment where animals live. Deforestation is destroying the environment where animals live.

- Choose an animal that is at risk in your country.
- Describe the natural environment of the animal.
- Is the animal a predator? If so, what is its prey?
- Is the animal a prey? If so, what is its predator?
- What negative effect are people causing to make this animal at risk?
- Describe how the animal is at risk.
- Suggest how people can change their behaviour to make the animal safe again.

Work in pairs or small groups. Collect the information. Prepare a three-minute presentation to share your findings with the class.

Check your progress

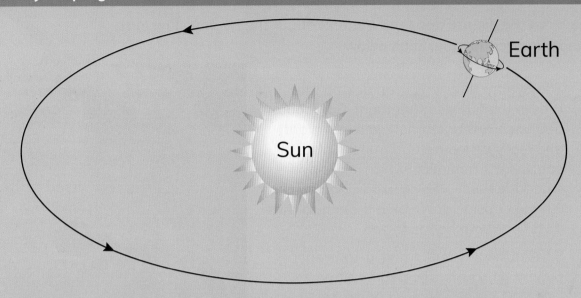

1 a Identify the two movements of the Earth shown on the diagram.

b How long does each movement take?

c Which two factors cause the seasons?

2 Here are some data for sunrise and sunset times for Kingston, Jamaica.

Date	Sunrise		Sunset
1 January	06:38		17:43
4 January	06:39		17:45
8 January	06:40		17:47
12 January	06:41		17:50
16 January	06:42		17:52
20 January	06:42		17:55

a Calculate the length of day for each day on the table.

b Describe the pattern of change in the length of day.

c Which season do you think Kingston is having in January?

d Which season will Kingston have in six months' time? Explain why.

Continued

3 Look at the picture and read the text about the pygmy slow loris, then answer the questions below.

The pygmy slow loris is an animal that lives in the forests of Vietnam, Cambodia and Laos. It is nocturnal (active at night) and feeds on leaves and fruits. It also eats insects and mice, which it kills by smacking them with its hands. Sometimes it hangs upside down on a branch so that it can use both hands to eat.

Snakes, eagles and orang-u-tans eat pygmy slow loris. The pygmy slow loris poisons its enemy. It has a patch of venom under each elbow. When a predator approaches, it licks the venom and spreads it over its teeth. Then it bites the predator.

The pygmy slow loris hibernates for short periods during autumn and winter.

a Describe the environment where the pygmy slow loris lives. Use the words 'hot' or 'cold', 'wet' or 'dry', 'forest' or 'grassland' in your answer.

b Identify two adaptations to this environment that the pygmy slow loris has.

c What adaptation does the pygmy slow loris have to kill its prey?

d What adaptation does the pygmy slow loris have to hunt at night?

e What are the pygmy slow loris's predators?

f Describe the adaptation the pygmy slow loris has to avoid being killed by its predators.

g What does the pygmy slow loris do when it hibernates?

h When does the pygmy slow loris hibernate?

i Why do you think the pygmy slow loris hibernates for short periods?

New science skills

Taking appropriately accurate measurements

How to measure the temperature of a liquid

We measure temperature in standard units called degrees Centigrade (°C).

When you measure the temperature of a liquid you must be careful to hold the thermometer correctly.

Look at the picture.

1   Hold the thermometer at the top. Make sure that the bulb of the thermometer does not touch the container. If the bulb touches the container it will measure the temperature of the container and not the liquid.

2   Wait until the red liquid in the thermometer stops moving.

3   Read the scale before you take the thermometer out of the liquid.

4   Line up your eye with the top surface of the red liquid in the thermometer to read the scale.

5   The temperature of the liquid in the picture is 43°C.

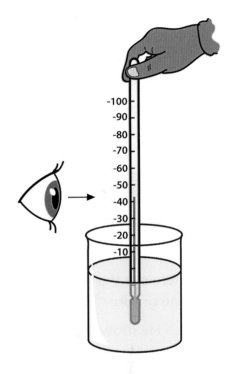

How to measure the volume of a liquid

We measure volume in standard units called millilitres (ml) or litres.

There are one thousand millilitres in one litre (1000 ml = 1 litre).

The most accurate way to measure the volume of a liquid is to use a measuring cylinder.

1   Pour the liquid into the measuring cylinder.

2   Put the measuring cylinder on a flat surface, like a table.

3   Line up your eye with the top surface of the water in the cylinder, as shown in the picture. Note that the water surface curves upwards.

4   Read the volume on the measuring cylinder at the bottom of the curve. The volume in the picture is 30 ml.

Presenting results

How to draw a line graph

A line graph is a good way to show how something changes over time. We plot the independent variable on the x-axis and the dependent variable on the y-axis.

Marcus measures the temperature of the air outside at different times of the day. He uses a thermometer to measure the temperature at 06:00, 09:00, 12:00, 15:00, 18:00 and 21:00.

He records his results in a table:

Time	06:00	09:00	12:00	15:00	18:00	21:00
Temperature °C	8	10	18	20	16	12

He wants to present his results in a line graph.

Here are the steps he takes to draw his line graph:

1   He draws the axes. The x-axis (horizontal) shows the time of day because time is the independent variable.

The y-axis (vertical) shows the temperature. This is the dependent variable which changes according to the independent variable.

He starts with 0°C. To make the highest temperature he recorded (20°C) fit on the axis he chooses a scale of 1 cm represents 2°C. This means he must draw his y-axis just over 10 cm high.

2   He labels the axes.

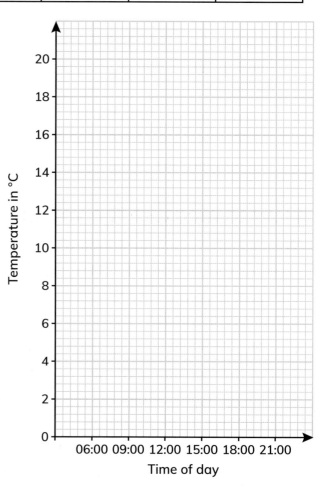

3 To make it easier to plot the points on his graph, Marcus uses a ruler to lightly draw a pencil line upwards from the time value on the *x*-axis (06:00) to the measured temperature value on the *y*-axis for that time (8°C).

He then places his ruler on the temperature measurement, 8°C, and draws a line across to the 06:00 line. He draws a cross where the two lines meet.

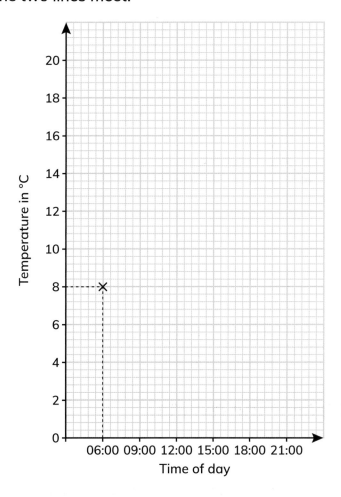

4 He plots the rest of the temperatures in the same way.

5 He uses a ruler to draw a line joining each of the crosses.

6 He writes a heading (title) above the graph.

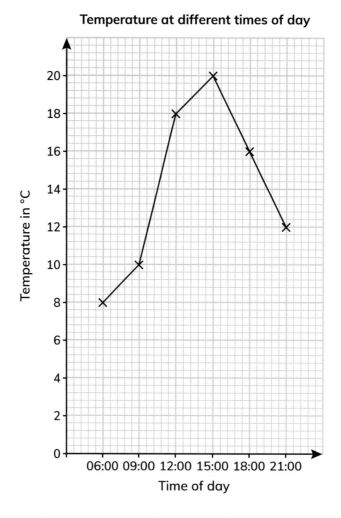

Temperature at different times of day

How does the graph present the results?

When we look at Marcus's graph, we can easily see trends or patterns.
For example:

- The temperature rises slowly from 06:00 to 09:00 and from 12:00 to 15:00.

- The temperature rises quickly in the morning from 09:00 until 12:00.

- The temperature falls quickly in the afternoon from 15:00 to 21:00.

Glossary and Index

small intestine	the organ that breaks down the partly digested food from the stomach into very tiny particles that can be absorbed into the blood	89
soluble	is able to dissolve (for example, sugar is soluble because it can dissolve in water)	79
solute	the solid that dissolves in a solution	79
solution	a mixture usually made of a solid dissolved in a liquid (the word is also used to mean the solving of a problem, or a correct answer)	79
solvent	the liquid part of the solution in which the solute dissolves	79
sound level meter	a hand-held device to measure sound	39
South Pole	the southernmost points on the globe	138
spongy	like a sponge with lots of holes in it that can be filled with air or water	18
spores	similar to seeds but always very small, used for reproduction in mosses and ferns	5
stamen	the male part of a flower	6
steam	heated water vapour	65
stigma	the tip of the carpel	6
stomach	the organ which mixes chewed food with digestive juices to form a thick liquid	89
streamlined	a smooth, sleek shape to reduce air or water resistance and achieve maximum speed (for example, a shark has a streamlined shape so that it can swim very fast)	114
stringed instrument	an instrument that is played by plucking the strings, such as a guitar or by using a bow across the strings, such as a violin, a cello or a double bass	49
structure	how the parts of something are arranged or put together, for example the roots, stem and leaves make up the structure of a plant	59